English Comes Alive!

Dynamic, Brain-Building Ways to Teach ESL and EFL

Jim Witherspoon, Ph.D.

See *www.englishcomesalive.com* to learn more about the topic or to e-mail the
author.
Synapse Books, 3201 Woodcrest Drive, Bryan, TX 77802

Editors: Judi Hermann and Becky Witherspoon

ISBN: 0-9838-2241-7
ISBN-13: 9780983822417

Dedication

To my colleagues and students in China, Hungary, Lithuania, and America

CONTENTS

INTRODUCTION

What events from life do you best recall? Was it your first date, or your first day of teaching, or 9/11, the day terrorists crashed into the World Trade Center? We strongly remember dramatic, unusual events—there's no question here—so why not use drama and variety to reinforce our teaching?

Research confirms the neural detail. Rats and people develop more nerve cells and nerve cell branches in their brains when they are exposed to dramatically different activities and social interaction. Because these nerve cells carry memory, we teachers want our students to have more of them. So we should teach diverse topics, exciting topics, in our ESL and EFL classes, and prod our students to interact.

What topics are diverse and exciting? Try games, songs, role playing, creative speeches, and humor—methods you probably use now, but here you will find more. Have your students tell stories, learn verbs by acting them out, identify objects pulled from a bag, correct amusingly erroneous sentences, read letters to Santa Claus, march with the Duke of York, and discuss great issues. Engaged by such activities, students chatter away in English, forgetting their fears and inhibitions.

So let's build memories! If you like vigorous teaching with lots of student-teacher interaction—keep reading.

Chapter 1.
ALERT THEM WITH THESE

Here are lively, get-moving activities that will keep your students motivated. For best results, shift promptly from one distinct activity to another. You might start with singing, for example, go next to pronunciation, and continue with role playing—whatever is appropriate for the level of your class.

Most of these activities require talking. It's the key to learning language—whether in toddlers or adults. The act of talking removes the fear of talking. And the more our students talk, the more fluent they become.

So take a look. Examine these many ways to rouse your students, to keep them talking, to give them confidence, to make them fluent.

Sing. Singing provides a great opening for individual classes or, better yet, for a group of combined classes. Begin each day with two or three lively songs from Chapter 3, Sing It. The simple words of these songs often repeat themselves, making them easy to remember.

Start Stories. Begin a story. You may say, for example, "It was a dark and stormy night." Then have each student contribute a few sentences to keep the story going. The last student concludes the story. See Chapter 5, Start Stories.

Slap Thighs, Snap Fingers, Say Words. To promote the learning of words in a category—such as food, jobs, or clothing—use rhythm. Have students slap their thighs twice, snap their fingers twice, and take turns saying different items within the category. Using food, for example, the group slaps and snaps and the first student says "cabbage" or another food. Then the group slaps and snaps and the second student says a different food. Continue slapping and snapping around the circle until students can no longer think of another food.

Correct These Sentences. Say or write humorously incorrect sentences for your students to correct, for example, "Us teachers never make mistakes" and "There bats flew out to greet them." See other examples in Chapter 8, Correct These Bloopers.

Move Right. Are your students sleepy? If so, seat them in a circle and say, "If you've already done some specified activity today, move to the next chair on your right." For example, you may ask, "Did you comb your hair this morning?" or "Did you drink coffee today?" Next have the student on your right ask a similar question. Continue until all students have asked one or more questions. Because students are seated in a circle and will have done different activities, they will soon be sitting together on the same chairs.

Do Role Playing. This works especially well for advanced classes. Write various situations on notepapers, for example, "Your grandmother drives a car but her vision is poor. Tell her that you think it's time for her to stop driving." Hand out the papers to your students who will then act out the situations described. In the situation here, one student takes the role of the grandchild and the other, the grandmother. See Chapter 6, Play Roles.

Urge your students to be dramatic. For the example, the grandmother may pretend to steer her car carelessly while the grandchild rides with her. The grandchild might then excitedly point out that the grandmother is driving over curbs and into bushes or through a red light.

Speak for One Minute. Put a list of concealed topics in a pile, and have each student draw one. This will be the topic of a one-minute speech. As soon as the students draw their topics—or after one or two minutes preparation—have them start speaking one by one.

Give the students humorous or unusual topics, such as (1) how to kiss, (2) the invention I am now working on, (3) the strangest thing I have ever seen, (4) how I made my first $1,000,000, (5) the novel I am now writing, (6) my years as a spy, (7) my first test of a newly invented time machine, (8) my encounter with space aliens, (9) my connection with the American President, and (10) my studies of chimpanzees in Africa.

Another day, ask students to speak about unusual or exciting events that have occurred during their real lives.

Prepare a Personality Poster or Bag. To get your students better acquainted, ask each to prepare a "personality poster" or "personality bag." Read the details in Chapter 20, Give Homework.

Sing and Dance the Hokey Cokey. Do your students need a wake-up call? Try this. Have them stand in a circle as they sing these words and do the corresponding actions: "You put your right hand in; you put your right hand out; in, out, in, out, you shake it all about. You do the Hokey Cokey and you turn yourself around. That's what it's all about, HEY!" (Simultaneously clap when you shout HEY!) Then repeat the song while giving other commands, such as "left foot in," "right hip in," "elbows in," "whole self in," and so on. Ask the students to contribute new lines to the song.

The words and directions here are for the British version of the song, and they continue with a chorus: "Whoa-o, the Hokey Cokey; whoa-o, the Hokey Cokey; whoa-o, the Hokey Cokey; knees bent, arms stretched, Rah! Rah! Rah!" I suggest that you omit the chorus while in the classroom, giving more emphasis to the naming of body parts. But if you have a game day outside, include the chorus. It's fun!

To hear the music and see the motions, search youtube.com for "Hokey Cokey" or for its slightly different American alternative, "Hokey Pokey."

Read Letters to God and Santa Claus. For laughs, insights, and learning, have students read aloud from *Children's Letters to God* (compiled by Stuart Hample and Eric Marshall) and *Children's Letters to Santa Claus* (compiled by Bill Adler). You may buy copies of these books online, for example, at amazon.com or amazon.co.uk or bn.com. Here are samples:

"Dear God, I went to this wedding and they kissed right in the church. Is that OK? Neil"

"Dear God, Did you mean for the giraffe to look like that or was it an accident? Norma"

Who Stole the Rice? Perhaps you already know the chant, "Who stole the cookie from the cookie jar?" It's a lively way to introduce words and to introduce new students to each other. But you may also use it to practice pronunciation of difficult sounds, such as r, w, and th, as described in Chapter 4, Pronounce It. Here's a sequence for the r in rice:

Teacher and Class: Who stole the rice from the fried rice bowl?

Teacher: (Name a student) stole the rice from the fried rice bowl.

Student: Who, me?

Teacher and Class: Yes, you.

Student: Couldn't be!

Teacher and Class: Then who?

Student: (Name another student) stole the rice from the fried rice bowl.

Continue the chant until all students get named or until you are ready for another activity.

Find Candy. Have two or more students leave the room while the others hide two or more pieces of candy in one location. Then have the two or more students seek the candy as the other students direct them by saying "hot" or "cold" to indicate how near they are to the candy. Repeat this procedure for other groups until all students have found some candy.

What Is It? Have students take turns describing items for the other students to identify, such as water. A student might say, for example, "You can drink it, splash it, and swim in it."

What's in the Bag? Bring a bag or box of concealed objects to class, for example, a comb, toothbrush, soap, pencil, pen, magnifying glass, spoon, cup, paper clip, magazine, book, and apple. Have the students identify them as you pull them out, and tell what we do with them.

When finished, drop all of the objects back into the bag or box. Then ask the students each to list what is there. Have the student with the longest list write the items on the board. Ask the other students to add anything missed.

Pass Ball from Neck to Neck. Several days after your class begins, ask your students to pass a sponge ball or other object from neck to neck. They bow their heads to grip the ball between the chin and the neck. The donor says, "I pass this ball to. . . ." The recipient says, "I receive this ball from. . . ." This activity generates laughter and gets the adrenaline flowing. Use it after some less interesting, more serious activity, as a means to get the students alert again.

Do Total Physical Response. This activity works exceptionally well for beginners. Give a command as you perform a simple action. Then have the students repeat the command as they perform it. Begin, for example, by rising from your chair as you say "stand." Immediately have the students rise from their chairs and say "stand." Then sit as you say "sit." Immediately have the students sit and say "sit." Repeat these commands two or three times before doing and saying others, such as "clap," "laugh," and "walk to a window." See Chapter 11, Act Out Words, and Chapter 12, Act Out Sentences, for similar ideas.

Demonstrate Verbs. Give each student or pair of students a verb or group of verbs to demonstrate and describe without using the names of the verbs. Then have the other students guess the verbs. Sometimes students will not know a verb you assign them. If so, tell them the definition before they demonstrate it.

For beginning classes, choose such words as stand, walk, and laugh. For advanced classes, choose such words as hop, whistle, and wave. See Chapter 11, Act Out Words.

On another day, have the students demonstrate verbs or nouns of their own choosing. If you wish, have them also use these verbs or nouns in sentences in the past, present, and future tenses.

Practice Pronunciation. Notice what American or British words or sounds your students have difficulty pronouncing. Then practice saying these words or sounds frequently. In Hungary and Lithuania, for example, many students mispronounce the w, v, and th sounds. If your students also have trouble pronouncing w words, ask them to say "water, wear, what, where, were, we, we're, world," and the like. Then ask them to say, "World Wide Web" and "Where were we?" and "What did we wear?"

See Chapter 4, Pronounce It, for other examples. See also Chapter 3, Sing It, for pronunciation practice in "They Think That They Heard Thunder" and other specially written songs.

Discuss It. Have students answer such questions as "What makes a happy family?" and "How will the world solve its energy needs for the future?" See Chapter 7, Answer and Discuss, for a list of suggested topics. Also discuss other matters—schools, homes, dating and marriage, clothing, business, music, movies, health, sports, technology—whatever appeals to your class.

Pass Over and Under. To learn the words "over" and "under," have your students form a line. Give a ball to the student at the front of the line. Have this student say OVER as he or she passes the ball over and behind his or her head to the next student in line. The next student says UNDER as he or she passes the ball between his or her legs to the next student. Continue saying OVER and UNDER while swinging the ball over the head and under the legs to the end of the line.

Alternatively, form two teams with the same number of students on each team. Have the teams compete in passing the ball over and under as quickly as possible to the ends of their lines.

Match Parts of Quotations and Words. Give each student a notepaper with part of a quotation. Next have the students match their parts with the parts given to other students. One student, for example, might have, "You can," and another student would complete it with, "if you think you can." Then have the pairs of students explain the meanings of their quotations. See Chapter 9, Match Quotations.

Also try matching parts of individual words, for example, teach er, doc tor, let ter, and stu dent.

Chant Duke of York. Rhymes, such as this, help students remember the meaning of words. First write the words on the board or project them on a screen. Next join the students in reading the words aloud. Then add actions to reinforce the meanings. For example, have the students pretend to march up and down a hill, then stand for "when they were up" and squat for "when they were down." The Duke of York may also be sung to the tune: A Hunting We Will Go.

The grand old Duke of York,
He had ten thousand men;
He marched them up to the top of the hill,
And he marched them down again.
And when they were up, they were up,
And when they were down, they were down,
And when they were only half-way up,
They were neither up nor down.

Describe Pictures. For this activity, you need first to collect some large, colored photographs or paintings, such as those you find on calendars and in the National Geographic Magazine. Cut out the interesting pictures, concentrating on those with unusual features, such as a man sitting in a bathtub reading a newspaper.

Bring enough of these pictures to give each student one picture. Put all the pictures face up in front of them, and let each student choose a picture to describe for the class. Later have the class tell a continuous story from a group of pictures, as described next.

Tell Continuous Stories from Pictures. This is the challenging part, the fun part for students who have enough vocabulary. Choose pictures that have obvious connections. Hand them to the students in the order you desire or, to stimulate more thought, let the students rearrange the pictures in the order they desire. As you or they do this, keep the pictures face up in a place where all can see them. Next have the first student start a story based on the first picture, the second student continue the story based on the second picture, and so on. In each case, have the students connect the previous picture with the next in their story telling. The last student concludes the story.

For advanced classes that have tried one or more continuous stories from selected pictures, turn a different set of pictures face down. Then have each student blindly choose a picture. Put these pictures out in the disconnected sequence they were chosen, and have the students tell a continuous story from them. They may gasp when first given this challenge, but they will get the job done.

As a final activity on another day, choose weird, seemingly unconnected pictures from which your students tell their continuous stories. For example, I sometimes include one of an ape drinking tea, a woman smelling the armpit of a man, and dinosaurs racing across a field. For such pictures, students must greatly stretch their imaginations and vocabularies.

Read Nursery Rhymes and Poems. Have the students read nursery rhymes or poems aloud, and discuss them. See Chapter 14, Read Rhymes.

Learn Idioms. Write idioms on the board one by one, and have your students decipher their meanings. Then have them use the idioms in sentences. Here are three to get you started: lemon (something defective), raining cats and dogs (a heavy rain), and get up on the wrong side of the bed (wake up in a bad mood). See more in Chapter 15, Learn Idioms.

Experience Shipwreck. Pretend that the class is in a boat in the South Pacific. A storm blows the boat onto a reef where it sinks. Each member of the class has time to save one person and one object to take ashore on a nearby, uninhabited island. Ask who and what each student wants to save, and why. List these items on the board. After all students have answered, ask each how long he or she would choose to stay on the island before being rescued.

Describe Others. Have each student describe another student in the room. Have the other students guess who is being described.

Who Am I? Seat two students in front of the board facing the group. As the students face forward, write the name of a famous person on the board, for example, Albert Einstein, William Shakespeare, Julius Caesar, Michelangelo, Charles Darwin, Marie Curie, Mother Teresa, Barack Obama, Vladimir Putin, or the name of a major leader in the country where you teach. Then have the two students ask questions which the other students answer, leading the two students to identify the famous person. Continue by using other names and other students who ask questions to identify famous persons.

Alternatively, put nametags of famous people on the backs of all your students, and have the students mingle. Each student then asks questions of the other students to find his or her identity.

What Nation am I? Do as above. Seat two students in front of the board. Write the name of a country on the board, for example, Mexico, China, or the United States. Then have the two students ask questions which the other students answer, leading the two students to the name of the country.

What Job Do I Have? Do as before. Seat two students in front of the board, facing the group. Write an occupation on the board behind these students, for example, teacher, doctor, or artist. Have the two students ask questions of other students to identify the job.

Play Hangman. Ask a student to think of a word having six to eight letters (or four to six letters for beginners). Then have the other students guess the letters. Each time they get any correct letter, the selector of the word writes it on one or more of the six to eight (or four to six) spaces for the word. Each time they miss, the selector draws part of a gallows and a stick-figure man hanging from the gallows. The class tries to guess the word before the selector completes the gallows and stick figure.

Whisper from Ear to Ear. Whisper this sentence or a similar sentence in the ear of your first student: "I saw Phil tickle Maria during our class yesterday." The first student whispers this message to the second, the second to the third, and so on. The last student tells the message aloud. Compare the final message with the original message.

Name Components of Words. Give each student a word, such as "hospital," from which he or she slowly names components, such as "doctors," "nurses," "patients," and "beds." The other students then guess the original word as quickly as possible.

Rhyme Words. Say a short word with which to rhyme another word, such as "cat" with "rat." Have each student attempt to rhyme a word with the original word. When a student cannot think of a rhyming word, he or she thinks of a new word with which to rhyme other words. Continue repeatedly around the circle of your students. This activity stimulates their minds and causes them to listen closely to different sounds.

Match Parts of Comic Strips. Cut out halves or thirds of Sunday or daily comic strips written in English. Give each student part of the strip. Then have the students match and show others the completed strips, and briefly tell what the strip describes.

Alternatively, give copies of entire strips to students to read and discuss. Make sure the message and vocabulary are easy enough to understand.

Simon Says. Give directions, but ask students to respond only when you precede the directions with "Simon says." For example, if you say, "Simon says, 'Touch your elbow,'" all students should do so. If you say instead, "Touch your elbow," no students should do so. Rapidly repeat several of the following, with and without "Simon says": pat your head, stick a finger in your ear, scratch your belly, tickle your neighbor, slap your thighs, touch your hips, laugh, smile, throw a kiss, wink your eye, rub your knee, clap your hands, and so on. Once you have given such directions, have your students take turns giving similar directions.

For variety and laughs on another day, have the students continue to hold a first position as they assume a second position, then a third position, and so on until it becomes physically impossible to go further. Thus the group may be patting their heads with one hand while sticking a finger in an ear with the other and hopping about on one foot.

Do Debates. Ask your students to prepare arguments for or against a controversial topic. Tell them the topic, randomly assign each student to a team, and let the team members consult for several minutes. When ready, have each student present part of the argument, allowing only 60 seconds per person. When both teams have finished, have them ask questions of first one team, then the other. Finally, have them tell their true positions. Here are some possible topics: (1) watching TV is a waste of time, (2) we need to build more nuclear reactors, (3) building the economy is more important than cutting pollution, (4) violence is sometimes justified, and (5) the government should block cell phones when they are used to coordinate looting and arson.

Arrange Colors. For beginners learning their colors, cut out identical squares of red, yellow, blue, white, black, orange, green, purple, and gray. Give identical sets of these colored squares to each student. Now have the students hold up each of the colors as you name them. Then have the students arrange the colored squares in particular sequences and patterns as you give directions.

Arrange Shapes. Before class, cut out six to ten different shapes of different colors from heavy paper. Make identical sets of these shapes, one set for each of your students.

In class, teach the names of the different shapes and colors before asking the students to arrange them. For example, you may separately draw or hold up a red oval, green triangle, and blue rectangle for them to identify. Also, teach them the different positions, such as right, left, above, below, and next to.

When ready, give each student an envelope containing a set of colored shapes. Then seat the students in chairs placed back to back. Ask one student in each pair of back-to-back students to arrange the shapes in a pattern, describing each arrangement for the partner to duplicate. The partner can hear the description of what to do but cannot see what is being done. The first student may say, for example, "Place the red circle above the blue square," and so on. When finished, the two partners look to see whether they have the shapes in the same positions. Then have the students reverse roles.

Alternatively, you give the directions. Tell all of your students where to place the different colors and shapes.

Draw from Directions of Another Student. Put students in pairs back to back. Have one student in each pair draw something—such as a robot or cartoon animal—and describe it for the other student to copy unseen. Then reverse roles.

Do Word Association. Have a first student say a word. Then have a second student say a related word, and so on, around the circle of students.

List Words from Seven Letters. Have the students tell you seven letters, including some vowels. Then have each student or pair of students list as many words as possible in three minutes, using these seven letters to make the words.

Is It an Animal? Ask one student to think of an animal, plant, or other item for the other students to guess. Go from student to student, allowing each to ask a question which the original student may answer with "yes" or "no." Continue until the students guess the unknown item.

Find Words in a Grid. Have the class call out 16 letters that you arrange in a grid on the board with four letters on each of four lines. Then ask the students in pairs to write as many words as possible by connecting the letters in the grid. They may connect them vertically, horizontally, diagonally, or in a zigzag, provided that each two letters lie next to each other. Allow three or four minutes for the groups to write their words. Then have one member of the group with the most words write them on the board. Here is an example of such a grid:

```
W H F L
E A L R
D E A U
F T B S
```

Students may spot such words as wed, whale, half, let, feat, as, us, rat, bat, ear, and so on, in this grid.

Next ask the entire class to call out words with connected letters that the first group failed to see.

What Do You See? Hold up an orange or another object. Ask what the students see. Then ask them to use their imaginations and tell what else they see. Perhaps they will imagine an orange tree or the color orange or a warmer climate or vitamin C or orange juice. Have the students pursue their thoughts. Then do the same with a cup of coffee, book, or other object.

Tell Time. Discuss how Americans tell time, for example, 10:15, 10:30, 10:45, and 10:50 a.m. (or 10 till 11:00) and 2:00 and 3:00 p.m.

Practice Greetings. Ask students to explain the meanings of various greetings, and then practice them. Include the following: hello, hi, good morning, good afternoon, good evening, good night, good-bye, so long, see you later, and have a good day. Then do the usual greeting and response, "How are you? I'm fine."

Notice that the reply to "How are you?" in America is almost always positive. The answer, in this case, is "I'm fine" or "Fine" or "Great" or a similar positive statement. After saying "I'm fine," many people ask the original greeter the same question, "And how are you?" or simply "And you?" The response again is, "I'm fine."

For adults, you may also want to show and practice a handshake and hug.

Please, Thank You, Welcome, and Excuse Me. Well educated people are polite. Ask your students the meaning of please, thank you, welcome, and excuse me, and how they would use them in ordinary conversation.

Define Survival Words. Write these words on the board and ask for definitions: entrance, exit, no trespassing, restrooms, poison, emergency, danger, caution, flammable, out of order, detour, railroad crossing, signal ahead, one way, and yield.

Discuss Holidays. Talk about some or all of the following: New Year's Eve, Valentine's Day, Easter, Independence Day, Halloween, Thanksgiving, and Christmas. If you do all of them, split the lesson into two or three days. As you mention each holiday, have your students name and briefly describe major holidays in their countries that occur at about the same time. End by jointly singing Christmas songs and by having your students read aloud *Children's Letters to Santa Claus* by Bill Adler, or *The Night before Christmas* by Clement Moore. See Chapter 18, Let's Celebrate.

What Is It? Ask each student to draw a picture of an animal or other object while the rest of the class tries to guess it in one minute.

Pretend. Have students in groups of two to four pretend to be the following: (1) hens laying eggs, (2) dogs chasing cats, (3) monkeys in a zoo, and (4) firefighters going to a fire. Other students guess what each group is pretending. For more ideas, see Chapter 13, Let's Pretend.

Give Synonyms. For advanced students, say a sentence in which you include one word for which you want synonyms. You may say, for example, "The Grand Canyon is awesome!" Then ask your students to repeat the sentence but substitute synonyms for awesome. One may say, "The Grand Canyon is magnificent!" and the next, "The Grand Canyon is breathtaking!" Continue around the circle until your students run out of synonyms. Then start another sentence for which the students give synonyms. See Chapter 16, Think Synonyms.

Chant the Alphabet. Have beginning to intermediate students chant the alphabet and call out words. The teacher and students start by saying, "A, give me an A word!" As they say "give me an A," the teacher points to a student who says a word starting with A, for example, "apple." Then the first student and the group say, "B, give me a B word!" As they say "give me a B word," the first student points to a second student who says a word starting with B, for example, "boy." Thus the teacher and students continue through part or all of the alphabet.

Some students may need more time to think of words. If so, slow the pace and add clapping, as in "A (clap, clap), give me an A word."

Count Monkeys. Have beginning students practice counting 1 through 10 or, better yet, 1 through 100. For true beginners, start with the rhyme of "Five Little Monkeys" in Chapter 14, Read Rhymes.

Describe Travels. Have students describe parks, museums, and other interesting places they have visited or read about. In the United States, for example, they might describe the majestic Grand Canyon in Arizona, the geysers of Yellowstone National Park in Wyoming, the shows and rides of Disney World in Florida, or the vast Smithsonian Museum in Washington, D.C.

Go Outside. Students often learn English faster when teachers take them outside their usual classrooms. You may want to walk about town with your students, invite them to a potluck picnic, take them outdoors to play games, go on a field trip, organize a talent show, or bring them home with you. See Chapter 19, Go Beyond the Classroom.

Chapter 2.
PLAN IT

Use this plan only as a rough guide. You know the level of your students—beginner, intermediate, or advanced—and what works best for them, so you may need to make adjustments.

The schedule here is typical of the daily plan I use for intermediate to advanced English classes of eight to ten students in Lithuania, but it can be adapted for others. These classes usually meet for three hours. When they meet for only one or two hours, I include fewer activities.

Whatever you do, be brief. For most groups, spend only five to ten minutes on any given activity before moving to the next. Why five to ten minutes? Because most people—especially young people—have short attention spans. By switching promptly from topic to topic, you keep your group alert.

Students get fidgety in hours-long classes. To avoid this, I plan substantial breaks about once every hour. This gives them time to stretch, walk about, visit, use the toilet down the hall, or have a snack. For very long classes, I sometimes go with my students to a snack bar during one of the breaks. If the class is small enough, we sit and visit together at the same table as we have our coffee. What a wonderful, relaxed way to teach English.

In addition, I insert physical activities into the teaching every 10 to 20 minutes, for example, the slapping of thighs, snapping of fingers, and naming of items in a category, or the marching and up-and-down movements of the Duke of York. You will find many such activities in Chapter 1, Alert Them with These; Chapter 12, Act Out Sentences; and Chapter 13, Let's Pretend. Any movement helps, even that in seeking partners when trying to match parts of quotations (Chapter 9, Match Quotations). Students need such breaks from sitting, particularly after long lessons on grammar or discussions of serious, war-and-peace type issues. Whatever the plan, I insert rousing activities swiftly when I see my students daydreaming.

When planning lessons, I include more activities than I will likely use. If time runs out, I move the unused activities to the next day's lesson plan. And I vary the activities from day to day.

Because these activities are described elsewhere in this book, I will simply list them here and give a few words of explanation:

Sing Songs. Make any necessary announcements and hand out the song sheets. Then sing. See Chapter 3, Sing It.

Assign Homework and Discuss Yesterday's Homework. Assign an article for the students to read overnight, an article that the class will use for discussion the next day. After assigning today's homework, have them present or discuss the assignment they did yesterday. See Chapters 20, 21, and 22, Give Homework, Read Stories, and Read Easier Stories.

Tell a Story. Pass a ball from student to student as each student contributes one to several sentences to a story. See Chapter 5, Start Stories.

Who Am I? Write the name of a prominent person on the board for selected students to identify by asking questions. Repeat this with different names and other students. See Chapter 1, Who Am I?

Practice Pronunciation. Say the following words and have the students repeat them: the, three, thirty-three, them, that, thanks, thing, thunder, thirst, think, there, their, threw, and through. Continue with a tongue-twisting phrase or sentence, such as "three thick things." See Chapter 4, Pronounce It.

Match Halves of Quotations. Give each student part of a quotation to match with that of another student. Then have the students read and explain their quotations. See Chapter 9, Match Quotations.

Speak for One Minute. Have students draw different topics on which they will each give a one-minute speech. Give them humorous or unusual topics, such as "My Years as a Spy" or "The Invention I am Now Working On." See Chapter 1, Speak for One Minute.

Do Role Playing. Give each pair of students a piece of paper listing a situation in which they will play different roles. See Chapter 6, Play Roles.

Slap Thighs, Snap Fingers, Say Words. Have students slap their thighs twice, snap their fingers twice, and take turns saying different items within a category. See Chapter 1, Slap Thighs, Snap Fingers, Say Words.

Tell a Story from Pictures. Have each student choose a different picture. Then have them arrange the pictures in an order that lets them tell a continuous story. See Chapter 1, Tell Continuous Stories from Pictures.

Act Out Verbs and Nouns. Have each student choose and demonstrate two or three verbs or nouns for the rest of the class to guess. See Chapter 11, Act Out Words.

Read Rhymes. Have students take turns reading lines of poetry to the class. See Chapter 14, Read Rhymes.

Rhyme Words. Have students take turns rhyming one word with another, for example, cat with rat. See Chapter 1, Rhyme Words.

Discuss Family. Ask your students, "What makes a happy family?" See Chapter 7, Answer and Discuss.

Chapter 3.

SING IT

Singing provides easily remembered instruction for your class or a group of combined classes. Begin each day with two or three lively songs. Students quickly learn them, especially when they involve movement and repetition. The tunes and their words reverberate in their minds hours to years later, giving them further practice with English.

For beginning classes in English, choose mainly children's songs, such as "The Wheels on the Bus." Notice how the words of this song repeat themselves: "the wheels on the bus go round and round, round and round, round and round." And as the students sing "round and round," they rotate their hands in circles. Thus they quickly learn this song and a few dozen words, just as young children learn them. For other beginners' songs, check the list below and those in Chapter 14, Read Rhymes.

For intermediate to advanced students, choose songs having more vocabulary. We in America often sing such songs when gathered for social events or around campfires.

I've written special words for selected songs, words that emphasize pronunciation. To teach the pronunciation of "th," for example, sing "They Think That They Heard Thunder," and for "r," sing "Fried Rice! We Love Fried Rice."

For more songs, search google.com. Type keywords for the specific song you want or for categories, such as "children's songs," "scout songs," or "campfire songs." If instead you want to hear songs as you watch bodily movements, search youtube.com.

1. HAIL! HAIL! THE GANG'S ALL HERE

Hail! Hail! The gang's all here.
Never mind the weather. Here we are together.

Hail! Hail! The gang's all here.
Let the fun begin right now.

2. IF YOU'RE HAPPY AND YOU KNOW IT
[Do items shown in parentheses.]
If you're happy and you know it, clap your hands (clap, clap).
If you're happy and you know it, clap your hands (clap, clap).
If you're happy and you know it, then you really ought to show it,
If you're happy and you know it, clap your hands (clap, clap).

If you're happy and you know it, stomp your feet (stomp, stomp) . . . .

If you're happy and you know it, shout hurrah! (HURRAH!) . . . .

If you're happy and you know it, do all three (clap, clap, stomp, stomp, HURRAH!) . . . .

3. HEAD, SHOULDERS, KNEES, AND TOES (Tune: There Is a Tavern in the Town)
[Touch each of the body parts—head, shoulders, knees, toes, eyes, ears, mouth, and nose—as you sing this song. Once the students learn these parts, you may want to choose other parts for the song, for example, heart, intestines, lungs, and liver.]
Head, shoulders, knees, and toes, knees and toes.
Head, shoulders, knees, and toes, knees and toes,
And eyes and ears and mouth and nose,
Head, shoulders, knees, and toes, knees and toes.

4. THIS LITTLE LIGHT OF MINE
[Do items shown in parentheses.]
This little light of mine, I'm going to let it shine.
This little light of mine, I'm going to let it shine.
This little light of mine, I'm going to let it shine—
Every day, every way—going to let my little light shine.

Hide it under a basket, NO (shout NO and thrust your fist up-ward), I'm going to let it shine.

Hide it under a basket, NO (shout NO and thrust fist), I'm going to let it shine.

Hide it under a basket, NO (shout NO and thrust fist), I'm going to let it shine—

Every day, every way—going to let my little light shine.

Shine it over (name of city or state), YES (shout YES and thrust your fist upward), I'm going to let it shine . . . .

Shine it over the world, YES (shout YES and thrust fist), I'm going to let it shine . . . .

5. PACK UP YOUR TROUBLES (Tune: Pack Up Your Troubles in Your Old Kit Bag)
Pack up your troubles in your old backpack
And smile, smile, smile,
Take water and bananas for a snack,
Smile now that's the style.
What's the use of worrying?
It never was worthwhile,
So, pack up your troubles in your old backpack
And smile, smile, smile.

6. THE MORE WE GET TOGETHER (Tune: Did You Ever See a Lassie?)
The more we get together, together, together,
The more we get together the happier we'll be.
For your friends are my friends, and my friends are your friends,
The more we get together, the happier we'll be.

7. IT'S A LONG WAY (Tune: It's a Long Way to Tipperary)
It's a long way around our big world,
It's a long way here to there.
But we can cross it with our friendship,

With our talking and our care.
Good-bye isolation,
Hello, be aware.
It's a long, long way around our big world,
But we want to share.

8. THE ANTS GO MARCHING (Tune: When Johnny Comes Marching Home)
The ants go marching one by one, hurrah, hurrah.
The ants go marching one by one, hurrah, hurrah.
The ants go marching one by one,
The little ones stop to eat a bun,
And they all go marching down into the ground
To get out of the rain.

9. THERE'S A HOLE IN THE BOTTOM OF THE SEA
There's a hole in the bottom of the sea.
There's a hole in the bottom of the sea.
There's a hole. There's a hole.
There's a hole in the bottom of the sea.

There's a log in the hole in the bottom of the sea.
There's a log in the hole in the bottom of the sea.
There's a hole. There's a hole.
There's a hole in the bottom of the sea.

There's a bump on the log in the hole in the bottom of the sea . . . .

There's a frog on the bump on the log in the hole in the bottom of the sea . . . .

There's a fly on the frog on the bump on the log in the hole in the bottom of the sea . . . .

The frog ate the fly on the frog on the bump on the log in the hole in the bottom of the sea . . . .

10. SHE'LL BE COMING ROUND THE MOUNTAIN

[As you finish each verse, repeat the words and actions described at the end of the previous verses. For example, when you finish verse two, you will say "yee-haw!" while thrusting your hand upward, and then, "toot! toot!" while pulling the cord of a whistle. At the end of verse three, you will say "hi there!" "yee haw!" and "toot toot!" while making the appropriate motions.]

She'll be coming round the mountain when she comes: toot! toot! (pull whistle)

She'll be coming round the mountain when she comes: toot! toot! (pull whistle)

She'll be coming round the mountain; she'll be coming round the mountain;

She'll be coming round the mountain when she comes: toot! toot! (pull whistle)

She'll be driving six white horses when she comes: yee haw! (thrust hand upward)

She'll be driving six white horses when she comes: yee haw! (thrust hand upward)

She'll be driving six white horses; she'll be driving six white horses;

She'll be driving six white horses when she comes: yee haw! (thrust hand upward) toot! toot! (pull whistle)

Oh, we'll all go out to greet her when she comes: Hi there! (wave) . . . .

And we'll all have chicken and dumplings when she comes: yum! yum! (rub stomach) . . . .

She will have to sleep with grandma when she comes: (make sound of a snore) . . . .

11. ROW, ROW, ROW YOUR BOAT
[First sing this song as is. Then divide the group into halves and sing it as a round.]

Row, row, row your boat gently down the stream,
Merrily, merrily, merrily, merrily, life is but a dream.

12. MY BONNIE LIES OVER THE OCEAN
[Sing this normally at first. Then alternately stand or sit each time you sing a word beginning with B or b.]

My Bonnie lies over the ocean.
My Bonnie lies over the sea.
My Bonnie lies over the ocean.
Oh, bring back my Bonnie to me.
Bring back, bring back, oh, bring back my Bonnie to me, to me.
Bring back, bring back, oh, bring back my Bonnie to me.

13. WHEN YOU WORE A TULIP
When you wore a tulip,
A sweet yellow tulip,
And I wore a big red rose.
When you caressed me,
'Twas then heaven blessed me,
What a blessing no one knows.
You made life cheery
When you called me dearie,
'Twas down where the blue grass grows.
Your lips were sweeter than julep
When you wore a tulip,
And I wore a big red rose.

14. PEACE LIKE A RIVER
[Some teachers raise the pitch as they move from verse to verse, and some groups clap their hands in rhythm as they sing the last verse.]

I've got peace like a river,
I've got peace like a river,
I've got peace like a river in my soul.

I've got peace like a river,
I've got peace like a river,
I've got peace like a river in my soul.

I've got joy like a fountain, ...

I've got love like an ocean, ...

I've got peace, joy, love like a river, ...

15. THE WHEELS ON THE BUS
[Do items shown in parentheses.]
The wheels on the bus go round and round (rotate hand), round and round (rotate hand), round and round (rotate hand).
The wheels on the bus go round and round (rotate hand),
All through the town.

The horn on the bus goes beep, beep, beep (press horn), beep, beep, beep (press horn), beep, beep, beep (press horn).
The horn on the bus goes beep, beep, beep (press horn),
All through the town.

The wipers on the bus go swish, swish, swish (swish hand), swish, swish, swish (swish hand), swish, swish, swish (swish hand).
The wipers on the bus go swish, swish, swish (swish hand),
All through the town.

The people on the bus go up and down (move up and down), up and down (move up and down), up and down (move up and down).
The people on the bus go up and down (move up and down),
All through the town.

The babies on the bus go waa, waa, waa (wipe tears), waa, waa, waa (wipe tears), waa, waa, waa (wipe tears).
The babies on the bus go waa, waa, waa (wipe tears),
All through the town.

The parents on the bus go shh, shh, shh (put finger to lips), shh, shh, shh (put finger to lips), shh, shh, shh (put finger to lips).
The parents on the bus go shh, shh, shh (put finger to lips),
All through the town.

16. THEY THINK THAT THEY HEARD THUNDER (Tune: The More We Get Together)
They think that they heard thunder, heard thunder, heard thunder.
They think that they heard thunder, heard thunder do this: BOOM!
The three of them heard thunder. The three of them heard thunder.
They think that they heard thunder, heard thunder do this: BOOM!

17. WORLD WIDE, WEB WIDE (Tune: Daisy, Daisy, Give Me Your Answer Do)
World wide, Web wide, what would we like to do?
Watch Wild West shows with horses and wagons too.
We don't want our shows without them.
We want to have Indians too.
As in the Wild West, we want what is best,
We want westerns with Pawnees and Sioux.

18. FRIED RICE! WE LOVE FRIED RICE (Tune: Hail! Hail! The Gang's All Here)
Fried rice! We love fried rice.
Whatever the weather, we have our rice together.
Fried rice! We love fried rice.
Let us start our meal right now.

19. LARGE, LITTLE, TALL, AND SMALL (Tune: Head, Shoulders, Knees, and Toes)
Large, little, tall, and small, tall and small,
Large, little, tall, and small, tall and small,
Let us look at girls and boys and all,
Large, little, tall, and small, tall and small.

Chapter 4.
PRONOUNCE IT

How do you pronounce Volkswagen? We Americans often say VW, avoiding the full word. Germans instead say FULHKS-vah-gen: at least that's how it sounds to Americans. The v of Germans sounds like our f, and the w sounds like our v.

Many Europeans mispronounce the English w, v, and th sounds. Some say, for example, "Ve eat wegetables" and "Vorld Vide Veb." I had a student in Hungary, a travel agent, who was determined to correct his pronunciation of "World Wide Web." He watched how I shaped my mouth to say the phrase. Then he repeatedly did the same. Indeed, each morning when I said, "Good morning," he answered, "World Wide Web."

Many Asians mispronounce the r and l sounds. Some say, for example, "flied lice" instead of "fried rice" and "arone" instead of "alone."

Listen to your students speak to find these and other problems with pronunciation. Then help them with the correct pronunciation. Have them watch your tongue, lips, and teeth as you form words. Many of us enjoy these variations in the sounds our students speak—there's nothing wrong with an accent—but it's easier to understand English when people pronounce it correctly.

Directions for Pronunciation. During the first class meetings, say words, phrases, or sentences—such as "three thick things" or "fried rice"—and have the entire class repeat them. Have the students watch your tongue, lips, and teeth as you speak. Pronounce the words several times until most or all of your students get them right.

In later class meetings, say each word, phrase, or sentence, and have individual students separately repeat it. As needed, correct their pronunciations and have them try again.

W Sound. Say some of the following and have the students repeat them: warm, walk, wag, wagon, waist, waste, wait, wake, awake, walk, wall, was, wash, watch, water, wave, way, weigh, we, weak, week, wear, where, web, weep, well, went, were, wet, whale, wheat, wheel, which, wide, wife, wild, will, win, won, wind, wing, wire, wish, witch, with, wood, word, work, world, wrist, who, what, when, and why. World Wide Web. Where were we? What did we wear?

V Sound. Say some of the following and have the students repeat them: vacation, vacant, vacuum, vague, valid, valley, value, valve, van, vandal, vase, vast, vain, vein, vary, very, vegetable, vehicle, verb, verse, vest, vice, victory, view, vine, volume, and vote. We put violins, vases, and vegetables in the vacant van.

Th Sound. Say some of the following and have the students repeat them: that, the, three, third, thirty-three, than, them, then, thanks, there, their, they're, thick, thief, thin, thing, think, thirst, thorn, thread, threat, threw, through, throw, thrill, thrifty, thrive, throat, throng, thumb, thump, thunder, mother, father, death, and worth. Three thick things. There were thirty-three threatening thieves.

More Th Sounds and Similar Sounds. Say some of the following and have the students repeat them: tin, thin; team, theme; tick, thick; tug, thug; trash, thrash; tie, thigh; taught, thought; day, they; doze, those; dough, though; dare, there; death, debt; drum, thumb; close, clothes; sin, thin; and fourth, fort. Thirty-three thieves threw things at their fathers.

R Sound. Say some of the following and have the students repeat them: birth, dinner, drip, drop, here, hear, number, paper, race, railroad, rain, rat, rate, read, red, refrigerator, report, restaurant, result, rhyme, rhythm, ribbon, rice, right, rip, rise, river, road, rock, roll, room, root, rope, rose, rot, rough, round, row, run, serve, travel, tree, trip, trouble, turn, write, and right. Fred had fried rice. Three of us had French fries from the fridge.

More R Sounds and Similar Sounds. Say some of the following and have the students repeat them: air, ear; or, are; bear, beer; brick, bring; bright, brighter; brown, frown; care, car; chair, cheer; cry, fry; dare, deer; fair, fear; for, far; father, farther; mother, matter; other, over; rap, wrap; rare, rear; raw, law; rider, writer; row, low; travel, trouble; and wear, were. The rear wheel ran over the red rock.

L Sound. Say some of the following and have the students repeat them: land, language, lap, large, last, late, learn, least, leave, left, less, let, letter, life, light, like, line, lips, list, little, live, loan, lonely, look, love, low, and lucky; airplane, all, almost, along, alone, already, animal, black, blue, build, call, child, children, class, clear, close, cloth, clothes, cold, early, floor, flower, girl, glass, gold, English, family, feel, field, fill, flat, full, ill, late, plan, plants, really, several, sleep, small, still, table, tall, tell, usually, and yellow. Lou loves to learn English. The last girl left a lace-covered pillow.

A and E Sounds. Say some of the following and have the students repeat them: bad, bed; bag, beg; band, bend; jam, gem, gym; had, head; ladder, letter; lag, leg; later, leader; man, men; pack, peck; paddle, peddle; pat, pet; sad, said; sand, send; sat, set; and tan, ten, tin. Let the fat lady settle in her saddle. Dad had ten men sit on the sand.

I and E Sounds. Say some of the following and have the students repeat them: bind, bend; bit, bead; beat, beet, bite; chip, cheap, cheep; did, deed; jam, gym; ill, eel; fist, feast; grid, greed; lick, leak; lip, leap; litter, liter; pick, peek; side, said; sick, seek; sin, seen; and still, steal. The silly sweet seal seemed sick. Dig the big green beans out of the pit.

Practice Pronunciation by Singing. In the songs of Chapter 3, practice "They Think That They Heard Thunder," 'World Wide, Web Wide," "Fried Rice! We Love Fried Rice," and "Large, Little, Tall, and Small."

Who Stole the Thread, Website, or Rice? Here's a lively way to practice both pronunciation and the names of students. It's based on the traditional chant, "Who stole the cookie from the cookie jar?" If your students have trouble pronouncing th, for example, try this:

Teacher and Class: Who stole the thread from the thirty-three thieves?

Teacher: (Name a student) stole the thread from the thirty-three thieves.

Student: Who, me?
Teacher and Class: Yes, you.
Student: Couldn't be!
Teacher and Class: Then who?

Student: (Name another student) stole the thread from the thirty-three thieves. . . .

Continue the chant until all students get named or until you are ready for another activity.

If your students have trouble pronouncing w, try instead: "Who stole the website from the World Wide Web?" If they have trouble pronouncing r, try: "Who stole the rice from the fried rice bowl?"

Play Game of Pronunciation. During the last one or two weeks of class, have pairs of students list all the words they know that start with a particular letter or groups of letters. Choose those that are difficult to pronounce, for example, th, w, and r. Have all groups write as many words as possible during two or three minutes. Then have the team with the most words write them on the board as all students say them aloud. Have other students contribute words the first team overlooked.

Say Words that Rhyme. Students must listen to and pronounce words carefully when choosing words that rhyme. Start with a short word with which to rhyme other words, such as wet and vet or wit and bit or three and be. Have each student attempt to rhyme a word with the original word. Continue from student to student, giving each a chance to respond.

Record Voices. Ask each student to record three or four minutes of his or her voice, choosing any topic or topics to discuss. Have the students speak freely, not read. Then write or record corrections for their individual pronunciations. Discuss and practice these corrections privately with each student.

Listen and Speak Online. Here are some excellent online sites that provide voices for your students to imitate:

Activities for ESL Students at a4esl.org lets you scroll to Podcasts, then click one of its choices, such as ESL Videos.

BBC Learning English provides many choices and many voices at bbclearningenglish.com.

Howjsay at howjsay.com is a talking dictionary that pronounces the English words you type or click, defines them, gives examples of their use in sentences, and translates them into other languages.

Learning English at voanews.com lets you read news as you hear Americans speak it at a slower than usual pace. The reports are varied and superb.

Listen & Read at spotlightradio.net/listen has you read as you hear people tell stories at a slower than usual pace.

Starfall at starfall.com is designed for children and adults who know few or no words in English. Students may listen to and practice reading aloud the ABCs, short stories, and poems.

Chapter 5.
START STORIES

"To learn it, do it," said Roger Schank. And how better can students do and learn English than by telling stories. Start a fictional story with one of the openings listed below or with an opening of your own. Then have each student contribute a few sentences to keep it going. Usually I have students randomly toss a sponge rubber ball from person to person across a circle of chairs to indicate who speaks next. The last student concludes the story.

It was a dark and stormy night. . . .

Our class is walking in the woods where we see a dinosaur crossing our path. . . .

As our class reaches the mountaintop, we find a rope hanging from a cloud. . . .

You are running for a bus. You leap over a puddle and find that you are now floating in the air, free of gravity. . . .

In a dream, someone of the opposite sex approaches and says. . . .

It is a dark, moonless night, and as we walk past a cemetery we see. . . .

We are exploring a vast, previously unknown cave. As we turn into the large tunnel at the right, we see. . . .

As our group returns to our classroom after a break, we find a ghost talking to another ghost on his cell phone. He tells us to listen to them on our cell phones. What do they say?. . . .

We are at a carnival riding a roller coaster that suddenly jumps off its track. . . .

The year is 2100. Our class just arrived at a distant planet in a far-off galaxy. . . .

Our submarine just set a world's record for a deep dive. As we leave the submarine in our diving suits, we are surprised to see. . . .

Chapter 6.
PLAY ROLES

When using role play in or out of class, students often forget their fear of speaking. Once a teenage Lithuanian girl from an intermediate class introduced me to her girlfriend near the cathedral in Vilnius but, oddly enough, pretended that I was her boyfriend from America. She and her girlfriend spoke fluently in English for 10 to 20 minutes about this fictitious boyfriend. Such is the power of role play.

The ideal role play is informal, as it was for these teenage girls, but it works almost as well in the classroom, particularly if the conversation involves something colorful and unexpected.

To get started, write some of the situations listed below on note-papers, and distribute them to pairs of students in your class. Have each student perform one of the parts required for the situation described. Ask them to be dramatic. If a father cannot hear well, for example, the son or daughter must shout to get his attention. And he, being partially deaf, will sometimes confuse one word for another.

Here are the suggestions for role play:

Your father does not hear well. He often confuses one word with another. He says, however, that this is not a problem. Tell him gently but insistently that he must buy a hearing aid.

Your grandmother drives a car but her vision is poor. Tell her that you think it is time for her to stop driving.

Your waitress stumbles while bringing a bowl of soup to your table. The soup spills on your shirt or blouse and dribbles to the floor. What do you say?

There is a fly swimming in your soup. Tell the waiter and ask for a new bowl of soup.

You want to start a new business: renting elephants to builders in your hometown. But you need money to buy the elephants. Ask the surprised bank manager for a loan.

You give the hairdresser specific directions on how to cut your hair and dye it blond. He or she than cuts it much too short and mistakenly dyes it red. What do you say?

Call the phone company. Tell the operator that there is something wrong with your phone, making it difficult for you to hear. Try to get him or her to correct the problem.

You are nervous as you travel by plane for the first time. Worse yet, the plane starts bouncing violently as it goes through thunderclouds. The passenger beside you has flown often and tries to reassure you that there is no danger.

You are in a taxi. Before paying you realize that you left your money in your hotel. Explain this to the driver.

Your sink is leaking badly, pouring gallons of water onto the floor. You phone a plumber who says he can't come today. Convince the reluctant plumber that he must come now.

You and a stranger are at the same sale. The prices are 50% off. You find a beautiful blouse in your size. Just as you start to remove it, the stranger grabs it and says she saw it first. What do you say?

Your neighbor bakes a pie and puts it on the sill of an open window to cool. Soon after, your cat jumps on the sill and eats some of the pie. Both you and the neighbor see the cat as it finishes its meal. What do you say?

You are a teenage midget boy who introduces your giant girlfriend to our class. You and your girlfriend then tell us how you met, how you fell in love, and the advantages of a midget dating a giant.

You are a salesperson trying to sell a defective car to a cautious customer. What do you say?

Ask your hesitant girlfriend or boyfriend to marry you. Vigorously plead your case.

You are a doctor who mistakenly prescribes a stimulant for a patient who needs a depressant. When the patient returns to your office, he or she is very excited. What do you say?

Your neighbor turns the volume so high on the TV that you have trouble studying your lessons. You know from experience that this neighbor is quarrelsome and easily gets angry. Ask him or her to turn down the volume.

Your neighbor grows prize-winning tulips. He just imported and planted a new kind of tulip that he says will be the most beautiful of all his tulips. Your dog then digs up the bulb and starts to eat it as you both watch. What do you say to the dog and neighbor?

You buy a television set and find that it is defective. You return the set to the store, expecting an instant refund, but the clerk does not want to give back your money. What do you say?

You read a help-wanted advertisement seeking 35 cooks for a summer camp. You apply but the interviewer says the ad is wrong. The camp instead needs 1 cook for 35 people. Your only experience is as a Boy or Girl Scout cooking over campfires. What do you say to get the job?

You are trading pots and pans for beaver pelts at a rendezvous in Wyoming in 1840. The Indian Chief says he wants guns instead of pots and pans. What do you say?

You are a wife whose husband wants to give up the town life of St. Louis, Missouri, and join the covered wagons going westward in the 1850s. You don't want to leave. What do you tell your husband?

Chapter 7.

ANSWER AND DISCUSS

As the proverb says, "Involve me and I understand." Here you will involve your students in back and forth conversations on thought-provoking issues—the kind of issues that work especially well for mature students.

Directions for Beginning to Intermediate Classes. Write a short question on the board, for example, "What makes a happy family?" or "What do you daydream about?" Read it aloud or have a volunteer read it. Define any words that your students may not know, for example, "daydream." Then call for comments.

Directions for Intermediate to Advanced Classes. Outside class, write separate questions on notepapers for each member of your class. In class, have each student draw one of these questions from your hand. Then have them individually read their questions aloud and respond.

Alternatively, read aloud one or more questions from the pages that follow. Then call for comments. Encourage all students to speak on one issue or another.

Games for Intermediate to Advanced Classes. Groups of two to four students can practice English by playing either of these two games: *Ungame* or *Life Stories*. You may buy them at walmart.com or amazon.com or amazon.co.uk. They offer discussion questions similar to those used hereafter.

If you could change the world, how would you change it and why?

If you could give two qualities to a newborn baby, what would they be and why?

What book have you especially enjoyed reading? Why?

What writer, artist, scientist, or other famous person do you especially admire? Why?

What teacher has changed your life for the better? In what way?

What makes a happy family?

What makes a happy marriage?

What makes a happy classroom?

For what are you most thankful?

What is one of your fondest memories from earlier years?

What is freedom?

How important is English for people in your country?

How can we best bring peace to the world?

What makes you angry?

What makes you sad?

What do you daydream about?

With what famous person would you like to visit? Why?

How can you become friends with someone who doesn't speak your language?

What is or was your favorite subject in school? Why?

If you could give any gift in the world to our class, what would it be and why?

Are the people in your country different from people in the United States? If so, in what way?

How has your country changed in your lifetime? How do you expect it to change in the next five to ten years?

In what ways will the world change in the next 10 to 50 years?

What are your thoughts about emigration?

Why do we have dictators?

Who did Stalin deport to Siberia during his reign? Why them?

Why did Hitler exterminate Jews during World War II?

How will the world solve its energy needs?

How can we best provide work for people who need it?

What do you think of the police?

How can we best reduce crime?

What are terrorists? How can we best protect ourselves from them?

What do you like to do in your spare time?

What sport do you most enjoy? Why?

How can we best live long and happy lives?

What do you want to be doing in five to ten years? How do you plan to achieve this?

How can we best prevent pollution and destruction of our environment?

Is the world gaining more people than it can support?

How can we best provide food to those who are hungry?

What are your thoughts about Great Britain and the United States?

What has been one of your greatest successes in life?

Who is one of your favorite relatives? Why?

Where in the world would you most like to go on vacation? Why there?

Of the trips you have taken, which did you find most interesting? Why?

We have a time machine. If you and your family (or friends) could live at any time in any part of the world for one week, when and where would you go? Why would you make this choice?

What is it like after we die?

Would you like to live forever? Why or why not?

Would you like to travel in space? If so, where and why?

Is there intelligent life elsewhere in our universe?

Chapter 8.
CORRECT THESE BLOOPERS

Richard Lederer has an unusual hobby: collecting errors in English. He copies and publishes mistakes from student papers, newspapers, magazines, and other sources, giving teachers a ready list of linguistic goofs.

For a humorous break from your usual lessons, read some of these goofy sentences to your students, and have them correct the mistakes. If you like the samples, consider buying one of Lederer's books, for example, *Anguished English: an Anthology of Accidental Assaults upon the English Language*, at amazon.com or amazon.co.uk or bn.com. You won't regret it. Once you have the book, you can easily read new batches of erroneous sentences to your students often. They will gladly correct and learn from the mistakes of others.

Directions for Intermediate to Advanced Classes. Read or write the following sentences for your students jointly to correct.

Franklin died in 1790 and is still dead.

For those of you who have children and don't know it, we have a nursery downstairs.

Tired of cleaning yourself? Let me do it.

Because Lederer's books are copyrighted, I can only quote a few sentences here. That's okay. You may want to write your own erroneous sentences or to copy such sentences from the papers you grade. Meanwhile, here are others I've made up.

Us teachers never make mistakes.

There bats flew out to greet them.

Tell me where to meet on your cell phone.

I should have went to college.

Her and me dashed to our grammar class.

We don't have nobody there.

He gave it to my fiend and I.

Them guts was bloody.

Frankenstein and I are going to feast alone.

Napoleon was upsetted by his defeat.

I wander why she staired at my pink shoes.

Are we already to enter the black hole?

Could you advice us on which rocket to fly?

We Neanderthals each have too feet.

I got feet bigger than your feet.

Its time to call our snakes home.

I am looking after my key and billfold.

Their going to they're castle.

There ain't nobody here but us lords and ladies.

Though she lived her entire life in Japan, she was born in California.

According to the menu, sandwiches are $8.00, soup is $6.00, and children are free.

Yes, let's except the invitation to wash elephants.

Here's a peace of our piece proposal.

Let's right about what's write.

He poured fewer water into less cups.

We brought fleas at the flea market.

She literally flew out the door.

The sun don't shine in caves.

Did it rain on the dessert as you ate your desert?

We have hundreds of foreign students from other countries on our campus.

A total of nine pterosaurs flew to their nests at twelve midnight.

The students were assigned housework from their textbook.

I was so exciting when I heard Albert Einstein speak.

He took the doze of medicine and dosed off in class.

What an interested walk we had among the robots.

The monsters was squatting inside they're tent.

I yelped when the angel kiss me.

What had she been do when she tripped over the goat?

Chapter 9.
MATCH QUOTATIONS

Here students sort through parts of quotations, matching their parts with those of other students. This takes thought and a good knowledge of English. It works best, therefore, in intermediate to advanced classes.

Directions. Before class, write part of each quotation on one paper and the other part on another paper. In class, randomly distribute the parts of the quotations to your students. Have each student match his or her part with the missing part given to another student. If anyone needs help defining words or matching part of a quotation, give it.

When all have matched their parts, have the pairs of students read their quotations and describe their meanings.

Alternatively, select a group of these quotations to assign as homework. Ask your students to read them and for each person to choose one to talk about the next day.

For Intermediate to Advanced Classes:

You can…if you think you can. Norman Vincent Peale

A journey of a thousand miles…begins with a single step. Lao-tzu

Do to others…as you would have them do to you. Luke 6:30

To learn it,…do it. Roger Schank

A house without books…is like a room without windows. Horace Mann

The only way to have a friend…is to be one. Ralph Waldo Emerson

Our life…is what our thoughts make it. Marcus Aurelius

Do what you can,…with what you have, where you are. Theodore Roosevelt

When you are good to others…you are best to yourself. Benjamin Franklin

Let no one come to you…without leaving better and happier. Mother Teresa

He enjoys much…who is thankful for little. Thomas Secker

Strangers are friends…that you have yet to meet. R. Lieberman

Love is the only thing you can get more of…by giving it away. Tom Watson

Choose a job you like…and you will never have to work. Confucius

Anything in life worth having…is worth working for. Andrew Carnegie

If there is no wind,…row! Polish proverb

God helps…the brave. J. C. F. von Schiller

For Advanced Classes:

Enthusiasm…is at the bottom of all progress. Henry Ford

A merry heart does good…like a medicine. Proverbs 17:22

He has achieved success who has lived well,…laughed often, and loved much. Bessie Stanley

To do more for the world than the world does for you—…that is success. Henry Ford

We must learn to live together as brothers…or perish together as fools. Martin Luther King, Jr.

A cloudy day…is no match for a sunny disposition. W. A. Ward

Inspiration works best…when you do. Andrew V. Mason

I'm a great believer in luck…and I find the harder I work, the more I have of it. Thomas Jefferson

Chance favors…the prepared mind. Louis Pasteur

They conquer…who believe they can. Ralph Waldo Emerson

When spiders unite,…they can tie down a lion. Ethiopian proverb

There is no exercise better for the heart…than reaching down and lifting people up. John Andrew

No act of kindness, no matter how small,…is ever wasted. Aesop

Most folks are about as happy…as they make up their minds to be. Abraham Lincoln

When love and skill work together,...expect a masterpiece. John Ruskin

The road to success...is always under construction. Doug Doyle

The future...is purchased by the present. Samuel Johnson

The man who makes no mistakes...does not usually make anything. Edward J. Phelps

He that can have patience...can have what he will. Benjamin Franklin

Man cannot discover new oceans...unless he has courage to lose sight of the shore. Andre Gide

The way to be happy...is to make others so. Robert G. Ingersoll

He deserves Paradise...who makes his companions laugh. The Quran

A smile is an inexpensive way...to improve your looks. C. Gordy

By the work...one knows the workman. Jean de La Fontaine

Action...speaks louder than words. Mark Twain

If I have seen further,...it is by standing on the shoulders of giants. Isaac Newton

We can do anything we want to do...if we stick to it long enough. Helen Keller

A man never stands as tall...as when he kneels to help a child. Knights of Pythagoras

If a free society cannot help the many who are poor,...it cannot save the few who are rich. John F. Kennedy

Peace rules the day...where reason rules the mind. Wilkie Collins

You cannot shake hands...with a clenched fist. Golda Meir

Friendship is the only cement...that will hold this world together. Woodrow Wilson

Every artist...was at first an amateur. Ralph Waldo Emerson

Teachers open the door...but you must enter by yourself. Chinese proverb

Give a man a fish...and you feed him for a day. Teach a man to fish and you feed him for a lifetime. Chinese proverb

Apply yourself. Get all the education you can, but then do something. . . . Don't just stand there, make it happen. Lee Iacocca

Perhaps the most valuable result of all education…is the ability to make yourself do the thing you have to do, when it ought to be done, whether you like it or not. Thomas H. Huxley

The only difference between a good day and a bad day…is your attitude. Dennis S. Brown

Chapter 10.

PONDER THESE

Here are a few quotations for you teachers to consider and enjoy, quotations more directed to you than to your students. Hurrah for teachers!

Nine-tenths of education is encouragement. Anatole France

Tell me and I forget. Show me and I remember. Involve me and I understand. Chinese proverb

Students learn what they care about, from people they care about and who, they know, care about them. Barbara Harrell Carson

Education's purpose is to replace an empty mind with an open one. Malcolm Forbes

Children are like wet cement. Whatever falls on them makes an impression. Gaim Ginott

Never help a child with a task at which he feels he can succeed. Maria Montessori

We are all tattooed in our cradles with the beliefs of our tribe. Oliver Wendell Holmes

Too often we give children answers to remember rather than problems to solve. Roger Lewin

Education is a weapon, whose effect depends on who holds it in his hands and at whom it is aimed. Joseph Stalin

The important thing is not so much that every child should be taught, as that every child should be given the wish to learn. John Lubbock

Whatever you want to teach, be brief. Horace

Education is the transmission of civilization. Will Durant

To teach is to learn twice over. Joseph Joubert

A teacher who is attempting to teach without inspiring the pupil with a desire to learn is hammering a cold iron. Horace Mann

The mind is not a vessel to be filled, but a fire to be ignited. Plutarch

I respect faith but doubt is what gets you an education. Wilson Mizner

The illiterates of the 21st century will not be those who cannot read and write, but those who cannot learn, unlearn, and relearn. Alvin Toffler

These are not books, lumps of lifeless paper, but minds alive on the shelves. Gilbert Highet

Children today are tyrants. They contradict their parents, gobble their food, and tyrannize their teachers. Socrates

Chapter 11.
ACT OUT WORDS

Students think for themselves when they act out a word or phrase for others to guess. And it's fun! Here are suggestions on how to proceed.

Directions for Beginning to Intermediate Classes. Write easy words on notepapers, using one word per paper. Give each pair of students one or two of these words to demonstrate. If they need help understanding the words, help them. Let them use movements and sounds (such as laughing or animal sounds) but not the words being demonstrated. Have the other students guess the words.

Later have pairs of students choose their own verbs, nouns, animals, occupations, or other items to demonstrate.

Directions for Intermediate to Advanced Classes. Write a mix of easy and somewhat more difficult words on notepapers, and give one notepaper to each student or pair of students. Help any students who have questions about their words. Then have each of the individual students or pairs of students act out their words for the rest of the class to guess.

Alternatively, write the easy and difficult words on notepapers, putting them in groups of three easy words and three difficult words per notepaper. Divide the class into two teams. Give each team one notepaper with six words. If the teams need help understanding their words, help them. Then have each team separately demonstrate as many of their words as possible in 60 seconds while the students on the other team guess the words. This fast-paced game spawns interaction, movement, laughter, and learning.

Charades. If you want more ideas for ACT OUT WORDS, buy a game of charades or reverse charades at amazon.com or elsewhere. In charades, a single student acts out words for the class to guess. In reverse charades, class members or team members act out words for a single student to guess.

Easy Words for Beginning to Advanced Classes

Stand, sit, walk, run, fly, swim, dive, wave, clap, come, go, head, ear, eye, nose, mouth, neck, back, arm, hand, finger, leg, foot, toe, red, yellow, green, blue, black, white, count, 1, 2, 3, 4, 5, 6, 7, 8, 9, 10, hot, cold, dance, home, room, table, chair, window, desk, cup, drink, water, eat, food, smile, laugh, play, cry, sleep, sing, kiss, clap, type, touch, see, hear, kick, wash, fight, stop, hammer, saw, car, drive, street, write, pencil, pen, tablet, taxi, bus, train, airplane, square, circle, telephone, cell phone, television, radio, music, camera, computer, keyboard, Internet, e-mail, horse, cow, chicken, dog, cat, shirt, blouse, pants, jeans, skirt, dress, shorts, shoe, baby, girl, boy, man, woman, ball, basketball, coffee, tea, soup, banana, apple, orange, hello, hi, good-bye, tree, flower, yes, no, dollar, euro, money, school, teacher, book, up, down, left, right, outside, inside, key, glasses, knife, fork, spoon, restaurant, soup, salad, sandwich, hamburger, pizza, ice cream, comb, brush, doctor, dentist, nurse, police, please, thank you, good morning, and good night.

Difficult Words for Intermediate to Advanced Classes

Excuse me, welcome, groceries, breathe, dig, hum, erase, shake, knock, jog, snore, tickle, skip, pour, point, wink, frown, sweep, kneel, lock, mop, cut, cheer, step, squat, wring, whisper, hop, whistle, hum, spit, jump, bark, pull, march, crawl, drop, jump, bend, yawn, blow, push, smell, bite, lick, stretch, faint, giggle, beg, stumble, squeeze, hiccup, bounce, bump, rattle, pour, juggle, cover, vomit, call, limp, hide, skate, cook, bake, climb, swat, find, air, 11, 12, 13, 14, 15, 16, 17, 18, 19, 20, 21, 22, 30, 40, 50, 60, 70, 80, 90, 100, 200, 1000, peach, plum, cherries, strawberries, blueberries, grapes, watermelon, tomato, potato, beans, peas, carrots, onions, corn, beets, turnips, mushrooms, cucumbers, cabbage, lettuce, spinach, meat, beef, steak, chicken, fish, vegetables, fruit, cheese, dessert, cake, pie, milk, juice, pop, beer, wine, bread, cereal, bag, scissors, glove, hair, lips, throat, chest, back, elbow, wrist, abdomen, shoulder, waist, hip, thigh, knee, ankle, brain, heart, lungs, liver, stomach, intestines, sheep, pig, duck, rabbit, elephant, giraffe, monkey, snake, spider, belt, matches, candle, campfire, light, dark, light bulb, circle, oval, triangle, rectangle, shower, bath, toilet, mirror, napkin, pillow, pregnant, edge, below, above, over, under, behind, in, on, beside, toothbrush, shampoo, diaper, golf, soccer, football, baseball, volleyball, tennis, blindfold, flat, one-half, one-quarter, newspaper, paper, magazine, balloon, contact lens, afraid, collar, envelope, sleeve, fat, thin, mountain, hill, stairs, floor, coin, hungry, guitar, piano, drum, screwdriver, clown, umbrella, ceiling, pulse, picture, art, bicycle, kite, doorknob, coat, needle, strong, weak, pocket, ladder, clock, suitcase, pack, pet, tail, highway, road, sidewalk, living room, dining room, hall, bedroom, bathroom, garage, airport, train station, bus station, library, post office, bank, grocery, department store, pharmacy, museum, hotel, danger, caution, warning, bottle, postcard, letter, stamp, cost, button, breakfast, lunch, dinner, supper, exit, friend, waiter, Sunday, Monday, Tuesday, Wednesday, Thursday, Friday, Saturday, spring, summer, fall, winter, warm, cool, sunny, windy, God, pray, religion, science, mathematics, psychology, education, and business.

Chapter 12.
ACT OUT SENTENCES

If students mime a word or action, they will more likely remember it than if they simply read it from a dictionary.

Directions for Beginning Classes. Give a command as you perform a simple action. Then have the students repeat the command as they perform it. Begin, for example, by rising from your chair as you say "stand." Immediately have the students rise from their chairs and say "stand." Then sit as you say "sit." Immediately have the students sit and say "sit." Repeat these commands two or three times before doing and saying others, such as "smile" and "walk."

When your students are ready, continue to the more advanced commands listed hereafter, such as "Touch your head" and "Clap your hands."

Directions for Beginning to Intermediate Classes. Read aloud and perhaps write on the board some of the "Actions for Beginning to Advanced Classes" listed hereafter. Then ask the class to show what these mean. If none of them know, demonstrate, and have the students say and demonstrate what you have just shown them.

Directions for Intermediate to Advanced Classes. Write some of the following actions on notepapers. Give one paper to each student. Then have the students take turns reading aloud the actions that all students then perform. When necessary, help them with difficult words or phrases, such as "imitate" and "jumping jacks."

Actions for Beginning to Advanced Classes:
Take two steps forward.
Take one step backward.
Hop on one foot.
Hop on both feet.
Make a happy face.
Make a silly face.

Make an angry face.
Raise your hands above your head.
Clap your hands.
Stamp your feet.
Put your hands over your ears.
Clap your hands while stamping your feet.
Put your hands over your eyes.
Put your hands over your mouth.
Close your eyes.
Touch your head.
Touch your lips.
Touch your arm.
Touch your leg.
Touch your foot.
Stand on one foot.
Kick your feet.
Hold up two fingers.
Hold up five fingers.
Hold up ten fingers.
Shake hands with someone.
Hold your nose shut and start talking.
Show how to eat an ice-cream cone.
Actions for Intermediate to Advanced Classes:
Make a scary face.
Make a scary sound.
Stick out your tongue.
Swallow.
Try to touch your chin with your tongue.
Stand on the toes of one foot.
Stand on the toes of both feet.
Scratch your head.
Hum a song that all students are likely to know.
Shake hands with your neighbors on your left and right.
Hug yourself.
Snap your fingers.
Touch your neck.

Touch your knee.
Touch your elbow.
Touch both of your shoulders.
Put your right hand on your left thigh.
Put your hands on your hips.
Wave to someone.
Imitate someone crying.
Imitate someone snoring.
Do a dance step.
Do four jumping jacks.
Throw a kiss to someone.
While seated, raise your legs off the floor.
Wiggle your fingers and toes.
Stand, close your eyes, turn around twice, and (with your eyes still closed) point to your teacher.
Clap your hands behind your back.
Touch your chin to your knee.
Rub your belly.
Rub your belly while patting your head.
Pat your head while counting to ten.
Rub your belly while patting your head and counting to ten.
Skip in place while holding your hands above your head.
Quickly say "World Wide Web" three times.
Quickly say "three thick things" three times.
Quickly say "fried rice" three times.
Sing "Row, Row, Row Your Boat" in a high-pitched voice.
Pull both knees up to your chest.
Put the palm of your hand over your heart.
Meow and purr like cats.
Bark and growl like dogs.
Form a circle and all join hands.
Insert your right finger into your left ear.
Squat on the floor and start walking like a duck.

Chapter 13.

LET'S PRETEND

When we pretend or playact, we often exaggerate, for example, frowning and constricting our mouths more than usual as we pretend to eat lemons. The frowns and puckers highlight the key words—eat lemons—making them stick in our minds. So let's pretend.

Directions for Beginning to Intermediate Classes. Write some of these activities on the board and read them aloud as you demonstrate them. Then have the students repeat what you said and did.

Directions for Intermediate to Advanced Classes. Write some of these items on notepapers. Give one paper to each student. Then follow either of these options: (1) have individual students take turns reading aloud the activities that all students then perform, or (2) have individual students take turns performing the activities while the other students guess what they are doing.

Pretend you are eating a lemon.

Pretend you are eating spaghetti.

Pretend you are a bird flying from one tree to another.

Pretend you are a dog digging a hole.

Pretend you are a cat stalking a bird.

Pretend you are a hula dancer.

Pretend you are a magician trying to make the rest of the class vanish.

Pretend you are a juggler trying to keep three balls in the air at once.

Pretend you are a baby bird getting food from your mother's bill.

Pretend you are a trombone player marching in a parade.

Pretend you are a drummer marching in a parade.

Pretend you are a dog upset by another dog entering your territory.

Pretend you are kissing your girlfriend, boyfriend, or spouse goodnight.

Rise, take two steps forward, and pretend to sit on a chair that does not exist.

Pretend you are chewing bubble gum and blowing bubbles.

Pretend you are a child sliding down a sliding board.

Pretend you are a carpenter building a house.

Pretend you are pushing a wheelbarrow.

Pretend you are playing soccer.

Pretend you are playing basketball.

Pretend you are peeling a banana.

Pretend you are a dog scratching an itchy spot.

Pretend you are a conductor of an orchestra.

Pretend you are riding a bicycle.

Pretend you are riding a horse.

Pretend you are vacuuming a carpet.

Pretend you are shoveling snow.

Pretend you are hanging clothes in a closet.

Pretend you are a butterfly.

Pretend you are walking in a wind so strong that you are about to be blown off your feet.

Pretend you are jumping a rope.

Pretend you are shaving.

Pretend you are milking a cow.

Pretend you are a barber giving a haircut.

Chapter 14.
READ RHYMES

Children learn part of their language by listening to and repeating nursery rhymes and poems. The rhymes make words easier to learn and remember, so easy that many of us still recall the rhymes we heard and said as children. ESL and EFL students likewise can learn quickly by reading rhymes.

Directions for Beginning to Intermediate Classes. Give your students copies of the children's rhymes or write them on the board. Then have the students join you in reading one or more aloud. Define the more difficult words, such as monkeys, shadow, itsy-bitsy, and waterspout.

Directions for Intermediate to Advanced Classes. Have students read one or more poems aloud, for example, "It Couldn't Be Done" or "The Road Not Taken." Then ask what the poems mean. Also ask them to define words that some may not know.

Five Little Monkeys. Author unknown.

You may either read or sing this and, if you wish, add the movements described in the parentheses. If you want to see the movements for this song or any other, search youtube.com.

Five (hold up five fingers) little monkeys jumping (move your hand up and down) on the bed,

One (hold up one finger) fell off and bumped his head (hold your head with one hand).

Mama called the doctor (hold imaginary cell phone to your ear) and the doctor said,

"No more monkeys (shake an index finger) jumping on the bed!"

Four (hold up four fingers) little monkeys jumping (move your hand up and down) on the bed,

One fell off and bumped his head (hold your head).
Mama called the doctor (hold cell phone) and the doctor said,
"No more monkeys (shake an index finger) jumping on the bed!"

Continue with three, two, and one little monkey jumping on the bed.

My Shadow. Robert Lewis Stevenson
I have a little shadow that
Goes in and out with me,
And what can be the use of him
Is more than I can see.

The Purple Cow. Gelett Burgess
I never saw a purple cow;
I never hope to see one.
But I can tell you, anyhow,
I'd rather see than be one!

Star Light, Star Bright. Author unknown.
Children sometimes recite this when they see the first star or the planet Venus at dusk.
Star light, star bright,
First star I see tonight,
I wish I may, I wish I might
Have the wish I wish tonight.

Twinkle, Twinkle Little Star. Jane Taylor.
Children sometimes sing this verse as they gaze into the night sky:
Twinkle, twinkle little star,
How I wonder what you are!
Up above the world so high,
Like a diamond in the sky!
Twinkle, twinkle little star,
How I wonder what you are!

The Itsy-Bitsy Spider. Author unknown.

Parents sometimes teach their children to sing and use hand motions with "The Itsy-Bitsy Spider." Baby spiders climb waterspouts and other tall objects, and then let out their silk. The wind catches the silk, carrying the spider to a new location where it is more likely to find food and less likely to find competing spiders.

The itsy-bitsy spider went up the waterspout (use fingers to climb your opposite arm).

Down came the rain (wave fingers downward) and washed the spider out.

Out came the sun (move hands and fingers upward and outward) and dried up all the rain,

And the itsy-bitsy spider went up the spout again (use fingers to climb).

Pass It On. Henry Burton
Have you had a kindness shown? Pass it on.
'Twas not given for thee alone. Pass it on.
Let it travel down the years,
Let it wipe another's tears,
Till in Heaven the deed appears. Pass it on.

It Couldn't Be Done. Edgar Guest
Somebody said that it couldn't be done,
But he with a chuckle replied
That "maybe it couldn't," but he would be one
Who wouldn't say so till he tried.
So he buckled right in with the trace of a grin
On his face. If he worried he hid it.
He started to sing as he tackled the thing
That couldn't be done, and he did it.

Somebody scoffed: "Oh, you'll never do that;
At least no one ever has done it";
But he took off his coat and he took off his hat
And the first thing we knew he'd begun it.
With a lift of his chin and a bit of a grin,

Without any doubting or quiddit,
He started to sing as he tackled the thing
That couldn't be done, and he did it.

There are thousands to tell you it cannot be done,
There are thousands to prophesy failure,
There are thousands to point out to you one by one,
The dangers that wait to assail you.
But just buckle in with a bit of a grin,
Just take off your coat and go to it;
Just start in to sing as you tackle the thing
That "cannot be done," and you'll do it.

The Road Not Taken. Robert Frost
Two roads diverged in a yellow wood,
And sorry I could not travel both
And be one traveler, long I stood
And looked down one as far as I could
To where it bent in the undergrowth;

Then took the other, as just as fair.
And having perhaps the better claim,
Because it was grassy and wanted wear;
Though as for that, the passing there
Had worn them really about the same,

And both that morning equally lay
In leaves no step had trodden black.
Oh, I kept the first for another day!
Yet knowing how way leads on to way,
I doubted if I should ever come back.

I shall be telling this with a sigh
Somewhere ages and ages hence:
Two roads diverged in a wood, and I—
I took the one less traveled by,
And that has made all the difference.

Chapter 15.
LEARN IDIOMS

When we translate idioms literally, we get funny pictures in our minds. Imagine, for example, someone who is "all thumbs" or someone who is "catching a cold." So our students need to learn the real meanings of idioms.

Directions for Intermediate to Advanced Classes. Define "idiom" as a group of words that have a meaning different from that of the individual words or as a single word with an unexpected meaning, and give your students two or three examples from the list below. Then write a few idioms on the board, and have your students guess their meanings. If they guess wrong, tell them the actual meanings. Next ask your students to use these idioms in sentences.

If you would like to read more idioms and examples of their use, see *Dave's ESL Cafe* at eslcafe.com/idioms. When you get there, click meanings and examples.

Student Translations of Their Own Idioms. For variety, have students give word by word translations of idioms from their native language, and tell their meanings.

Idioms Used by Speakers of English

All thumbs (clumsy)

Back-seat driver (passenger who gives unsought advice to the driver)

Be broke (have no money)

Bend over backwards (try very hard)

Bite the dust (be defeated or die)

Blow it (fail at something)

Call a halt (stop doing something)

Call off (decide not to continue doing something)

Catch a cold (get infected with a cold virus)

Chicken out (give up because of fear)

Come again (say it again)
Couch potato (someone who sits hour after hour watching TV)
Crack the books (prepare by reading textbooks or other books)
Cut back (use fewer or less of something)
Down in the dumps (sad)
Egghead (highly intelligent person)
Fall in love (be extremely attracted to someone)
Feel blue (feel sad)
Figure out (find an answer)
Fishy (strange and suspicious)
For the birds (of little use or meaning)
Get off someone's back (stop disturbing someone)
Go all out (use maximal effort to achieve something)
Go to the dogs (deteriorate or get worse)
Goose bumps (tiny bumps on the skin resulting from cold or excitement)
Half-hearted (giving less than the best effort)
Hang in there (keep trying)
Hit the books (study)
Hit the hay (go to bed)
Hit the roof (get very angry)
Hot under the collar (angry)
Junk mail (unwanted mail mostly from advertisers)
Kick the bucket (die)
Lemon (something defective)
Let the cat out of the bag (tell a secret)
Monkey business (silly or dishonest behavior)
Mums the word (keep quiet about something)
New kid on the block (new member of a group)
Now and then (occasionally)
Nuts (crazy)
On pins and needles (nervous about something)
On time (at the scheduled time)
Pat on the back (praise)
Piece of cake (easy to do)
Pipe down (be quiet)

Play it by ear (respond as needed to a situation)
Pooped (tired or exhausted)
Prick up your ears (listen closely)
Pull someone's leg (fool someone)
Raining cats and dogs (a heavy rain)
Red tape (excessive paperwork to fill out)
Run down (fatigued and perhaps ill)
See red (become angry)
Sleep on it (continue thinking about something overnight)
Smell a rat (suspect that something is wrong)
Spill the beans (tell someone a secret)
State of the art (using the latest technology)
Step on it! (hurry!)
Take it easy (relax)
Take the bull by the horns (boldly do something)
Tie the knot (get married)
Tight spot (difficult situation)
Toot one's own horn (brag about something)
Under the influence (drunk)
Under the weather (sick)

Chapter 16.
THINK SYNONYMS

Writers love synonyms. Why? Synonyms make their writing accurate, colorful, and vivid—stirring the thoughts of their readers. Contrast "I would like to be a writer" with "I yearn to be a writer." The synonym "yearn" shows a passionate desire. Those who yearn to be writers will persevere till they get published.

Directions for Advanced Classes. Say a sentence in which you include one word for which you want synonyms. You may say, for example, "The Grand Canyon is awesome!" Then ask your students to repeat the sentence but substitute synonyms for awesome. One may say, "The Grand Canyon is magnificent!" and the next, "The Grand Canyon is breathtaking!" Continue around the circle until your students run out of synonyms. Then start another sentence for which the students give synonyms.

Alternatively, simply say the word for which you seek synonyms. Then have your students call them out. Continue with antonyms for the same word.

Here are some synonyms and antonyms to help you get started. Find others in your mind or in the thesaurus at merriam-webster.com.

Dynamic. Synonyms: active, effective, energetic, forceful, lively, peppy, potent, powerful, robust, vibrant, vigorous, vital. Antonyms: dull, feeble, impotent, inactive, ineffective, lethargic, listless, puny, weak.

Exciting. Synonyms: breathtaking, electrifying, exhilarating, galvanizing, hair-raising, rousing, spine-tingling, stimulating, stirring, thrilling. Antonyms: boring, dull, humdrum, uninteresting, unexciting.

Excellent. Synonyms: admirable, exemplary, great, first-class, first-rate, notable, matchless, peerless, preeminent, superb, superior, top-notch. Antonyms: bad, inferior, low-grade, poor, second-rate, substandard.

Happy. Synonyms: cheerful, contented, elated, glad, joyous, pleased. Antonyms: displeased, gloomy, sad, sorry, unhappy.

Interesting. Synonyms: absorbing, engaging, engrossing, enthralling, fascinating, gripping, riveting, stimulating. Antonyms: boring, drab, dull, monotonous, tedious, uninteresting.

Large. Synonyms: big, bulky, gigantic, good-sized, hefty, huge, massive, outsized, oversized, sizable, vast. Antonyms: diminutive, little, minute, pint-sized, small, tiny, undersized, wee.

Stimulate. Synonyms: activate, arouse, encourage, energize, excite, fire up, invigorate, jump-start, rouse, spark, pep up, vitalize. Antonyms: calm, dampen, deaden, discourage, soothe, subdue, tranquillize.

Chapter 17.

READ, SAY, AND CHUCKLE

Sometimes we teachers are as playful as our students. If you are one of these playful teachers, you may want to combine humor with pronunciation by giving your students this quiz. It ends with a phony Siamese sentence that translates, "Oh what a noisy person I am."

Directions for Intermediate to Advanced Classes. After your students have had considerable practice with pronunciation, print this page for them to do in class. Just before they start, have them say "three thick things" in a quiet voice and then a loud voice. Next have them say "World Wide Web" in a happy voice and then a sad voice.

If needed, revise this page to fit the pronunciation problems of your current students.

1. Read everything carefully before doing anything.

2. Write your name in the space above the previous sentence.

3. Draw a circle around each "th" in sentence four.

4. Whisper the following words: "the, them, that, throw, three."

5. Say in a soft but distinct voice: "The three of them heard thunder."

6. Draw a circle around each "w" in sentence seven.

7. Say the following words in a quiet voice: "we, will, watch, where, why."

8. Say in a quiet but angry voice: "We went to watch the thirty-three wagons."

9. Repeat in a sad voice: "We went to watch the thirty-three wagons."

10. Say this in a happy voice: "World Wide Web."

11. If you think you have followed directions to this point, say loudly, "I have!"

12. Say the following words in a louder voice yet: "three thick things."

13. Say slowly: "Thirty-three thieves threw thorns to the throng."

14. Say clearly: "I have followed all of the directions for the thirty-three thieves."

15. Say the following Siamese words loudly: "oh wha tah noy see purr suhn nigh am."

16. Say the previous Siamese words clearly in English: "Oh what a noisy person I am."

17. Now that you have finished reading everything, do only sentences one through ten. Please speak in a quiet voice in order not to disturb the other students.

Chapter 18.
LET'S CELEBRATE

Christmas: what a joyous, brightly lit holiday. We celebrate it and forget the fading sun of December, the darkest month in the northern hemisphere.

Directions. Talk about Christmas and, if time permits, about other major holidays in the United States: New Year's Eve, Valentine's Day, Easter, Independence Day, Halloween, and Thanksgiving. If you do all of them, split the lesson into two or three days. As you mention each holiday, have your foreign students name and briefly describe their holidays occurring at about the same time. End by jointly singing Christmas songs and by having the students read aloud, *Children's Letters to Santa Claus* or *The Night before Christmas*.

We Wish You a Merry Christmas
We wish you a Merry Christmas,
We wish you a Merry Christmas,
We wish you a Merry Christmas,
And a Happy New Year.

Good tidings we bring to you and your kin.
We wish you a Merry Christmas and a Happy New Year.

We wish you a Merry Christmas,
We wish you a Merry Christmas,
We wish you a Merry Christmas,
And a Happy New Year.

Go, Tell It on the Mountain
(Chorus) Go, tell it on the mountain,
Over the hills and everywhere.

Go, tell it on the mountain,
That Jesus Christ is born.

While shepherds kept their watching
Over silent flocks by night,
Behold throughout the heavens
There shone a holy light.

Repeat Chorus

Down in a lowly manger
The humble Christ was born,
And God sent us salvation,
That blessed Christmas morn.

Repeat Chorus

Letters to Santa Claus

For laughs, insights, and learning, have students read aloud from *Children's Letters to Santa Claus*, compiled by Bill Adler. You may buy this inexpensive book online, for example, at amazon.com or amazon.co.uk or bn.com. Here are sample letters:

"Dear Santa, I have been a good boy all year and all I want for Christmas is a magic trick that will make my sister disappear. Love, Andrew"

"Dear Santa, Last Christmas you left me a sled. This Christmas please leave some snow. Your pal, Jed"

The Night before Christmas

St. Nicholas (later called Santa Claus) is the patron saint of children, the person now known for delivering gifts to them at Christmas. His physical appearance and behavior changed in the 1820's to match those described by Clement Moore in *The Night before Christmas*. Moore's poem has flying reindeer landing on rooftops and a chubby St. Nicholas dropping down chimneys to deliver the gifts.

If you have students read this story aloud, ask them to be dramatic. Have them nestle in their beds, throw open the window, whistle to reindeer, fly to the housetop, drop down the chimney, open a pack of toys, smoke a pipe, wink an eye, fill the stockings, go up the chimney, and fly away.

Consider buying a large, colorfully illustrated child's book of *The Night before Christmas*. If you do, have the students show the illustrations as they read from the book.

'Twas the night before Christmas, when all through the house
Not a creature was stirring, not even a mouse.
The stockings were hung by the chimney with care,
In hopes that St. Nicholas soon would be there.
The children were nestled all snug in their beds,
While visions of sugarplums danced in their heads.
And Mamma in her 'kerchief, and I in my cap,
Had just settled down for a long winter's nap.
When out on the lawn there arose such a clatter,
I sprang from my bed to see what was the matter.
Away to the window I flew like a flash,
Tore open the shutters and threw up the sash.
The moon on the breast of the new-fallen snow
Gave the luster of midday to objects below.
When, what to my wondering eyes should appear,
But a miniature sleigh, and eight tiny reindeer.
With a little old driver, so lively and quick,
I knew in a moment it must be St. Nick.
More rapid than eagles his coursers they came,
And he whistled, and shouted, and called them by name.
"Now Dasher! Now Dancer! Now Prancer and Vixen!
On Comet! On Cupid! On Donner and Blitzen!
To the top of the porch! To the top of the wall!
Now dash away! Dash away! Dash away all!"
As dry leaves before the wild hurricane fly,
When they meet with an obstacle, mount to the sky;
So up to the housetop the coursers they flew,
With the sleigh full of toys—and St. Nicholas too.

And then in a twinkling, I heard on the roof
The prancing and pawing of each little hoof.
As I drew in my head, and was turning around,
Down the chimney St. Nicholas came with a bound.
He was dressed all in fur, from his head to his foot,
And his clothes were all tarnished with ashes and soot.
A bundle of toys was flung on his back,
And he looked like a peddler, just opening his pack.
His eyes—how they twinkled! His dimples: how merry,
His cheeks were like roses, his nose like a cherry.
His droll little mouth was drawn up like a bow,
And the beard of his chin was as white as the snow.
The stump of a pipe he held tight in his teeth,
And the smoke it encircled his head like a wreath.
He had a broad face, and a little round belly
That shook when he laughed, like a bowl full of jelly.
He was chubby and plump, a right jolly old elf,
And I laughed when I saw him, in spite of myself.
A wink of his eye and a twist of his head,
Soon gave me to know I had nothing to dread.
He spoke not a word, but went straight to his work,
And filled all the stockings, then turned with a jerk,
And laying his finger aside of his nose,
And giving a nod, up the chimney he rose.
He sprang to his sleigh, to his team gave a whistle,
And away they all flew like the down of a thistle.
But I heard him exclaim, ere he drove of sight,
"Happy Christmas to all, and to all a good night."

Chapter 19.

GO BEYOND THE CLASSROOM

We ask our students to evaluate their classes each year. Thus we can later remove or modify activities that work poorly and emphasize those that work well. The last question in 1996 was, "What did you like best about the course?" One of our students surprised us by answering, "The intercourse after dinner."

Yes, we had intercourse—that is, we conversed with our students twice weekly as we walked through the city of Vilnius, Lithuania. These were optional get-togethers, something we did outside our classrooms, so we usually had just ten to fifteen students come for a pleasant hour or more of walking with five or six teachers. Notice the ratio. Only two or three students walked with each teacher, and they occasionally shifted from one teacher to another, getting exposure to different accents.

As we walked, our students described the surroundings they knew so well, showed us the parliament building where some had defended their country from threatening tanks, told us their thoughts and feelings about many subjects, and asked question after question. Think about it. Can there be any better way to learn English? Can there be any better way to become fluent speakers?

So I urge you:

Walk and Talk with Your Students. Give them the option of joining you and perhaps other students and teachers outside the classroom. Give them the chance to speak freely, to show what they know, to ask all the questions they want. You'll never regret it.

Picnic Together. Picnicking works almost as well as walking and talking. So, why not invite all of your students and perhaps their families to a potluck picnic? Mothers can come more readily if they bring their kids. Ask your students to bring food and drinks to share, and tell them that you will too. If you have a spouse and children who speak English, invite them. The more English speakers, the more your students will learn.

Play Games. If your picnic site lacks entertainment, bring your own. Play one or more games before or after a meal. Here are suggestions:

Sing and Dance the Hokey Cokey. You may already have sung the Hokey Cokey in class, but you probably skipped the chorus. You'll want it now, but let's review the verses first. Have your students stand in a circle as they sing and dance the following: "You put your right hand in; you put your right hand out; in, out, in, out, you shake it all about. You do the Hokey Cokey and you turn yourself around. That's what it's all about, HEY!"

Now continue with the chorus: "Whoa-o, the Hokey Cokey; whoa-o, the Hokey Cokey; whoa-o, the Hokey Cokey; knees bent, arms stretched, Rah! Rah! Rah!" For the chorus, you and the students join hands in the circle and run toward and then away from each other each time you sing, "Whoa-o, the Hokey Cokey." Next you bend at the knees and then stretch upward as you sing, "knees bent, arms stretched." And finally you thrust your fists repeatedly upward as you sing, "Rah! Rah! Rah!" This is all quick moving and physical. You and your students will bump shoulders as you run toward the center.

As you continue with the song and its chorus, give other commands. Say "left foot in," "right hip in," "elbows in," "whole self in," and so on.

To hear the Hokey Cokey and see its motions, search for it at youtube.com.

Toss Water-filled Balloons. To prepare, fill spherical balloons with water, one balloon for each pair of students. Fill extra balloons in case any break.

When ready, give each pair of students a balloon. Then have the entire class form two lines about five feet apart with the partners standing face to face across the two lines. Now tell the group to start tossing their balloons back and forth to their partners. This should be easy for everyone, but if any balloons break at this stage, replace them.

After a few tosses, tell the participants to back up several feet, and keep tossing. As the minutes pass, separate the lines farther yet until balloons start to explode and release water. Continue until you find which pair of participants can toss their balloon the farthest without it popping.

Race with Legs Roped Together. To prepare, find two or more ropes or other ties to bind the legs of your students together. Test these by tying your right leg to the left leg of another person. Then cooperatively walk in unison to reach and go around some target. This is what you will later have your students do.

When ready, form two teams with each team having several pairs of participants. Show the pairs how they are to tie their legs together. Then have the lead pairs for each team tie their knots. The other participants line up in pairs behind the lead pair.

Give a signal for the race to begin. The hobbled pairs start walking or running toward a target placed 20 to 25 feet away and equidistant from both pairs. The target can be a tree or post or beanbag or whatever you have. When the pairs reach the target, they circle it and return to their teams. Now the next pairs of students untie the bindings from the first pairs, retie them around their own legs, and race to and around the target. Continue this sequence to find the winning team.

Pass Ball Neck to Neck and Over and Under. If you have not previously used these two activities in class, do them now. The directions are in Chapter 1, Alert Them with These. To prepare, bring two balls for the two competing teams. Then line up the team members and have them pass the balls to find which team can do it quickest.

Take Field Trips. Here's another great way to speak informally with students and build rapport—take them on field trips, preferably out-of-doors, all-day field trips. In Hungary, for example, our teachers and students took an annual train ride from Eger to the Bükk National Park. There we hiked along streams, cataracts, and lakes, to a wide-mouthed cave, conversing in English as we went. In Lithuania, for another example, we took a train or bus to Trakai Castle, an awesome place set in the middle of a scenic lake. There we toured, picnicked, and sometimes sailed, talking back-and-forth in English throughout the day.

Have a Talent Show. Have students prepare a skit or songs for a talent show to be given on or near the last day of class. This works best if other classes do the same and meet in a large room for the presentations. Most classes perform very well. Some voluntarily write their own scripts and prepare colorful costumes.

Do an Overseas Exchange. If your students come from afar, consider a teacher-student exchange between your countries. Our faculty at Grand Canyon University did this for about 10 years with selected Hungarian students, and it worked wonderfully well. When the students came, we kept them in our homes and those of our friends. Then we drove them to such places as the Heard Museum, Apache Trail, Saguaro National Park, and Grand Canyon, speaking English wherever we went.

An exchange is a major, major event for such students. Some pay as much as two-thirds of a year's salary to make the trip. I spoke in 2011 with one of them, Judit Bota, who came with other students and a professor from Hungary to Arizona and California in 2001. She said, "It was the highlight of my life."

Chapter 20.
GIVE HOMEWORK

Assign enough daily homework to reinforce the teaching of English but not to interfere with other essential activities. Here are suggestions:

Prepare Personality Posters or Bags. Have your students prepare either posters or bags of items that reveal something about their personalities. This works best as an early assignment to help your students get acquainted.

1. *Personality Posters*. For this option, have the students paste, tape, or draw five or six pictures or similar items on a poster, and label them. Later, hang these on the wall for long-term display. Thus you and your students will have reminders of each other.

2. *Personality Bags*. For this option, have the students individually place five or six personal objects in a paper bag or other container.

Prepare your own poster or bag in advance to show the students approximately what you want them to do. On the day you assign the homework, point to items on your poster or take out your objects, and say what they tell about you. Days later, have your students do the same. Limit the number of students speaking each day. And for large classes, limit the number of objects described to three or four, not five or six.

Tell your students not to bring photo albums. These take too long to describe.

Assign Readings. Assign a short, simple story for the students to read overnight. As students read this story and others, they should use their dictionaries to look up words they do not know. The next day, have the students discuss what they've read.

I've written short, personal stories in Chapter 21, Read Stories, and Chapter 22, Read Easier Stories—most describing people and events in China, Hungary, and Lithuania. Some of the stories are uplifting, for example, "Why Not Be Cheerful?" Others are scary, for example, "Lithuania as Route to Siberia." Others yet are weird, for example, the story of "Qigong Doctors" who make their patients convulse. But all are informative.

I've also written three chapters specifically for teachers and students of education: Chapters 23 through 25, Build Their Brains, Love Them, and Get Enthused.

For beginning classes, you may instead prefer stories from children's books, such as those written by Dr. Suess and P. D. Eastman. These stories repeat one-syllable words in a dramatic, rhythmic way that makes them easy to learn. For students who know only a few dozen words in English, I suggest reading *Hop on Pop* or *Go, Dog. Go!* If instead you prefer guided reading on the Internet, try *Starfall* at starfall.com.

Travel with $10,000. Have groups of two to four students plan trips to any English speaking country or countries they would like to visit. Give them 10,000 imaginary dollars for the trip. Have them tell the class the next day how they plan to travel and what they plan to see.

Report News. Ask your students to prepare news reports on current events in their country or in the United States or elsewhere. The Voice of America at voanews.com works especially well for this. It lets students read as they listen.

Watch, Listen, Learn, and Speak. Use this assignment only for adults. Ask them to type the keywords "how to" at youtube.com. This will retrieve a large number of videos showing how to do this and that, for example, "How to Detect a Lie," "How to Juggle Three Balls," and "How to Use an Exercise Ball." Have each student watch a video, learn the procedure shown, and give a demonstration speech about it at the next class.

Because anyone can prepare videos for YouTube, your students will find some that are risqué. That's why this assignment is suitable only for adults in certain cultures. Search youtube.com yourself before deciding whether the assignment is appropriate.

Write a Letter. Ask each of your students to write you a letter. Then correct their English and return their letters.

Seek Advice. As homework, ask each student to write a personal problem, either real or imagined, for which he or she would like advice. Bring it to class where all students will exchange problems. As homework again, ask each student to write advice on how to solve the problem he or she got. Then have the students read their solutions aloud in class and perhaps seek further advice from their listeners.

Prepare Speeches. Ask students to prepare two to three minute talks on subjects of their own choosing.

Write Directions for New Activities. During the last week or two of class, ask each student to write directions for one or two new English-speaking activities for possible use in your classroom. They may find such activities by using google.com and the keyword ESL or by checking the websites listed in Chapter 27, Go to the Web. Then select the activities you want the class to try, and ask the authors to give directions.

Chapter 21.
READ STORIES

We each have unusual, enlightening, sometimes humorous stories forever printed in our minds. We tell them to our friends, and since you teachers are now my cerebral friends, I'm going to tell some to you—mainly stories about teaching overseas. If you want to use any as homework assignments for your students, you are welcome to copy them.

Directions. Assign stories from this chapter for intermediate to advanced students and, stories from Chapter 22, Read Easier Stories, for beginning to intermediate students. For others yet, see *EFL/ESL Lessons and Lesson Plans* at iteslj.org and *VOA Learning English* at voanews.

Packing Light

I once talked with a missionary who had made seven trips around the world. When I asked how much luggage he took, he said "only a small bag with a change or two of clothes." Each night he hand-washed the clothes he had worn that day and hung them up to dry.

Though I never learned to travel with so few clothes, I did learn to hand-wash them and to travel anywhere in the world with a single backpack. This simplifies getting on and off planes, through customs, and up and down stairs.

Plane is Broke!

That's what she said in poorly worded English, "Plane is broke!" Here we were in Beijing, 14 teachers, headed for our assignments in western China. The airline couldn't help. It could fly only two of us the following week. But Chinese friends came to our rescue, getting an entire first-class car added to a train going to Ürümqi, our destination, a train that would get us there in three-and-a-half days.

What a thrill to see 2,300 miles of China from the windows of a slow-moving train—everything from people to rice to camels. What a greater thrill yet to teach in Ürümqi and learn their customs. Did you know, for example, that the Chinese in 1988 drove at night without headlights, that the doctors successfully treated victims of stroke with waves of their hands, and that dorms and classroom buildings in Ürümqi were lined with spittoons? Some people thought spitting more healthful than swallowing. I taught physiology and learned these customs only because I had recently written a textbook, *Human Physiology*, and because a Vice President from Xinjiang Agricultural College saw it. In response, he invited me there.

As often happens, one adventure leads to another. Two of our English teachers became temporarily ill, so I taught their classes and loved it. This led me to train in English as a Second Language (ESL) and to teach English in Europe.

Speeding through Ürümqi
When we arrived in Ürümqi, China, those of us with doctor's degrees were put in cars and those without, were put in a bus. Then our driver sped through the city and through red lights—blaring his horn to clear the way.

Drivers, such as ours, steered to the center of the streets. Indeed, it was illegal to drive along the sides of low-traffic streets: that's where people, bikes, and donkeys went. Additionally, drivers honked their horns frequently and drove aggressively. The largest vehicle or the one with the noisiest horn seemed to have the right of way. And at night, they drove without headlights, only parking lights. Drivers flashed their headlights only when approaching other vehicles. Those were exciting days for the people who rode in cars, and more exciting yet for the people who dodged them.

Free Talk
While in China, our teachers gave a "Free Talk" every evening for anyone wanting to attend. Typically about 200 came. After the talks, they swarmed us, wanting to learn more about America and to practice English. We loved answering their questions, so we usually stayed another 30 to 60 minutes. Then they followed us to our dorm where we had to shut the door. Otherwise we could not have gotten our sleep.

Their questions included: What do you like most about China? Who will be the next U.S. president? How are the relations of whites with blacks in America? How can America prevent a nuclear war? And how do we arrange to study in America?

As we and the students got better acquainted, the questions got more personal for our young teachers. How do young people in America date and get married? Do you like me? Are you married? I think some of our students were entranced by their teachers. What do you think?

Feasting with Muslims

Muslim colleagues invited our entire group of teachers to four of their homes: one Kazakh, two Uighur, and one Hui. They were celebrating Korban, the religious holiday in which sheep or other animals were killed, cooked, and served with other foods at their overloaded dining tables.

The Kazakh home was that of Deputy Secretary Kahop (wrong spelling but phonetically correct). The Deputy Secretary, I think, was what we would call the Vice President of the Communist Party at our Xinjiang Agricultural College. Kahop was a warm-hearted, sturdily built man, about 50 years of age. As we ate his breads, mutton, and soup, Kahop told how he lived in a yurt (a tent home) until he was 16. He said the Kazakhs welcome other Kazakhs, even strangers, to their yurts for food and a night's rest.

The Kazakhs, I found, were a friendly, vigorous people who had trouble at times adjusting to new laws, such as the restrictions on family size. Most Chinese families were urged—through financial, school, and job incentives—to have only one child, and Muslim families, to have only two children. The Chinese thus limited the growth of their vast population.

At one of the Uighur homes, that of Vice President Hileemon (phonetically correct), we had several foods and watched Uighur dancing. Although Mrs. Hileemon is not Kazakh, she brought each of us a glass of fermented mare's milk to drink, the traditional drink of the Kazakhs. The college had been developing ways to pasteurize, package, and distribute such milk to Kazakhs living in Ürümqi. The milk was mouth-puckering sour, yet we drank it because we didn't want to offend our host. Another of the foods—a sort of wonton soup with mutton, tomato, and peppers—was good but fatty. Many of the people here consider fat a special treat.

At the home of the Hui, we had similar foods: soup, breads, cookies, nuts, raisins, watermelon seeds, and candies. Then we danced to Hui music. My wife and I jitterbugged (a quick-moving jazz dance), much to the delight of our colleagues and hosts.

Qigong Doctors

China was weirdly different from America at times—and medical treatment by qigong (pronounced chee-goong) was the weirdest. Our students urged me to observe it, this therapy and exercise that brought surprising, almost unbelievable relief from certain illnesses. So I got up early one day to meet two of the students at People's Park. The students introduced me to "master" teachers and practitioners of qigong, including one who tried (but failed) to put me in a trance. By waving their hands, the masters caused their subjects to jerk into odd positions.

One of the students then took me to a hospital where I met for two hours with a physician and his assistants who were using qigong. One of the patients said she had a stroke four years ago that left her paralyzed and unable to write. But the past month's treatments with qigong took away most of her paralysis. She gladly showed me how she could now write normally.

The head doctor then invited me to watch his assistant treat the woman. First, they had her lie backside down on a bed. Then the assistant covered her eyes and waved his hands at her body, soon causing her back to arch and her body to bounce up and down. While convulsing, however, she bounced precariously toward the edge of the bed. Seeing this, the head doctor, who had been talking to me, jumped up and began vigorously moving his hands and fingers back and forth toward the woman. This caused her to bounce back to the center of the bed, at which point the assistant again took over.

How do the qigong doctors cause convulsions and treat patients with waves of their hands? They say they project qi, connecting the sky to the earth through the patient's body, giving the body energy. But they too would like to know the less mystical, underlying mechanisms.

Yurts

Our hosts in China took us to Heavenly Lake (Tianchi) in mountains of 14,000 to 18,000 feet, peaks well above those of our Rocky Mountains in the United States. There we found yurts—large, circular felt tents—each containing a Kazakh family. The Kazakhs here were a nomadic, horse-riding people who moved their yurts two to four times yearly. By changing altitudes or sides of a mountain, they got optimal temperatures and year-round grazing for their sheep.

Walking ahead of the other teachers at Heavenly Lake, I reached three yurts overlooking a snow-capped peak. When I sat to enjoy the view, two Kazakh boys approached me. They knew only a few words of English, so we conversed with a mix of talk and gestures. One offered me a cigarette (which I politely refused) and an opportunity to sleep the night in their yurt. Unfortunately, I had to return to the college.

Communist Ice Cream

Let's shift to Hungary where our group taught English for eleven summers. In 1990, a professor from the University of Szeged invited us to an ice cream parlor on a dead-end street. We sat at a canopied table on the street itself, but the waitress refused to serve us. When the professor asked why, the waitress said that it had rained earlier and that to reach us she would have to cross a puddle at the curb.

Our host was incensed. She said that this response was typical of the old communist regime in which people were paid whether they worked or not. Then she herself stepped to the curb to show the young waitress how easily she could step over the water.

Free Ride for Wet Americans

We teachers ordinarily walked from our home to the college-prep gymnasium where we taught in Szeged, a distance of about two miles. One day five of us were caught in heavy rain as we walked home, so one of our teachers hailed a taxi. But this taxi and the next were full, so she jumped into a third as I ran up whistling for the other teachers.

The driver must have had children, and he spoke little English. We had to throw stuffed animals from the back seat to the window behind it to make room. Then we showed him a map and pointed to our home.

When we arrived, I pulled out money. "No," he said, "No taxi!" We had mistakenly gotten some generous, perhaps intimidated Hungarian to give us a free ride home.

Distorted History

Hungarians often watch American movies and TV. The movies give them both favorable and unfavorable impressions of Americans and sometimes a distorted view of history. One Hungarian seriously asked one of our teachers whether she had ever fought Indians. The Hungarian had no idea that our fighting had stopped nearly 100 years earlier.

Americans make similar or worse mistakes. One of our students spoke with a teenage American who thought Lenin Boulevard in Szeged was named for John Lennon of the Beatles, not for Vladimir Lenin of Russia. Lenin Boulevard, by the way, was renamed when the Russian troops left Hungary in 1991.

The Neanderthals

We took our Hungarian students by train most summers to the Bükk National Park—a large, wooded, mountainous area about 50 miles north of Eger. There we hiked through the woods past ponds and streams to a picnic spot where we ate our sack lunches. Then we continued to Istállóskö Cave. The students practiced their English as we rode the train, hiked, ate, and explored the cave.

The cave had long ago been the home of Neanderthals, as evidenced by the charcoal of ancient campfires, arrowheads made of bone, and the nearby bones of deer, bear, water buffalo, and mammoths. We could imagine the Neanderthals standing at the enormous entrance to this cave, planning their next attack.

Stale Bread

Part of our entertainment came from János, the driver of our van. He loved to be with us but spoke no English. To compensate, he used large sweeping gestures and banging of his hands to get across messages.

János and other Hungarians consider first-rate bread part of their heritage and, for all I know, it may be written in their constitution. Thus he was incensed one summer when a restaurant in Budapest served stale bread to our group. He complained both to the waitress and the manager who denied the bread was stale. When we returned to Eger, János wrote to the mayor of Budapest to explain the problem with the bread. As we learned later, the mayor had the restaurant inspected. The inspector found additional problems, so the mayor closed the restaurant. It no longer exists.

The People of Hungary

I was often asked, "What do you like most about Hungary?" I replied, "The people." I said the same about China and later, Lithuania. The towns and terrain were interesting, of course, but the people more so. Being so closely involved with my students—several hours every weekday and sometimes on weekends—I could not help but like them. Indeed, I liked everyone with whom we had frequent contact: faculty, secretaries, and others.

Why did I like them? I'll illustrate with Sandor Orban, the Rector of Esterházy Károly College, and his family. Sandor was my student in 1991. A year later he invited Becky (my wife) and me to join him and his nine-year-old son, Balázs, at the college retreat in Szentendre. Picture the busy rector, the head of the college, entertaining us, showing us the town of Szentendre, and cooking our meals. Picture his son playing checkers with us, teaching us Hungarian words, and leaning his head on Becky's shoulder. How could we not like such warm and generous people?

Sandor and his wife, Ági, also invited us year after year to their home where he cooked goulash—perhaps the best goulash in the world. Ági always offered wine with our dinner. Knowing the generosity of Hungarians, I once requested "fél kicsi" which translates as "half of a small amount." Ági laughed, fetched a baby spoon, poured a few drops of wine into it, and pushed it into my mouth.

Lithuania as Route to Siberia

Lithuania was scarier than Hungary. We sometimes took our students to the former KGB (secret police) prison in Vilnius, the capitol city. The younger, less informed of these students were horrified by what they learned.

Our guide in 1996 and 1997 was a former prisoner who had later been deported to Siberia. He was part of the resistance movement (those who fought Russian occupation) when he was captured and imprisoned. He described from experience the various methods of interrogation, torture, and punishment for disobedience. He showed us the small cells in which they were held—sometimes with only two prisoners per cell and other times with twenty or thirty. He showed us where they were forced to stand for hours over cold water into which they dropped if they fell asleep, where they were placed in a padded cell while listening to a constant buzz, where they were forced to sit on the edge of a chair while being struck on the back of the neck, where they had to sit, stand, or lie while facing always in one direction. Surprisingly, he showed no bitterness. He simply wanted to inform us.

This prisoner was one of 300,000 Lithuanians deported to Siberia between 1941 and 1953. Most were teachers, lawyers, politicians, and wealthy landowners. Why did Joseph Stalin, the Soviet leader, send these particular people to Siberia? And why were they underfed and overworked, causing many to die?

Tears for Stalin

My students, especially those born in the 1940s, said some of their classmates cried when Stalin died in 1953. Only later did they associate him with torture and deportation. They also spoke of schizophrenia in Soviet Lithuania. The schools taught a rosy view of communism and its history; their parents taught a different view.

Regarding war, they said all people in the Soviet Union were told that America wanted to start a war to destroy them. They said further that the Soviet war in Afghanistan in the 1980s depleted the Russian economy, weakening Russia's control of the occupied states. Otherwise the Russians would still govern Lithuania.

Pessimism vs. Optimism

My first students in Lithuania, the class of 1995, were professors, elementary teachers, and others well acquainted with the old Soviet Union. They were a dedicated but somewhat pessimistic group, pleased with their freedom to speak and travel but still worried about the economy and Russia. The worry ran historically deep. As we saw in shops and cemeteries, Christ Himself was depicted with a sad face, usually with head resting on hand, as if giving up on Lithuania.

In contrast to the despairing Christ and the glum-looking people on the streets—most of our students smiled and laughed. The positive outlook of their American teachers, they said, balanced their pessimism. One student, however, objected to our smiles. "The Lithuanian tradition," she said, "is to be sad and talk about it."

Our host for nearly two decades, Irena Navickienė, told me in 2001 that joy and optimism vary with age and experience. Her daughter, Živilė, she said, was optimistic because she had experienced mainly good times up till then, and that Živilė wanted Irena to become more optimistic. Irena herself claimed to be alternately optimistic and pessimistic, unable fully to escape her communist-dominated past. And her mother, she thought, would always be pessimistic, reacting to her past. There's probably truth here, but I had to look deeply to discern it. I knew each of these women well, knew they had suffered, but could only see three lovely, smiling ladies.

Conversation Then and Now

The fear of Russia and the KGB both inhibited and promoted conversation. In 1996, I had lunch with Irena Veisaitė, Chair of the Open Society Fund. She felt that she and her friends had better communication during Soviet times. They could not speak publicly, she said, so they met privately to discuss their feelings and philosophy. She didn't want to return to those years but was concerned that the watching of TV, use of the Internet, and overwork was interfering with conversation.

Change in Lithuania

The last of the Russian troops left Lithuania in 1993. It was then free. But when we came to visit that same year, we found Lithuania drab and poorly supplied. Indeed, the hot water in Vilnius, the capitol city, was turned off during the week we were there, and the stench at the meat market suggested little refrigeration.

Other Americans noticed shortages and responded with help. When we returned in 1995, we found 20 to 30 Peace Corps trainees at our hotel. They were learning Lithuanian and otherwise preparing to work in villages as they had done the past three years. Some would teach, some would build, and some would farm or do other jobs, depending on the need and their abilities. Additionally, I met a generous American who came, as we did, in 1993, and seeing the shortage of medical equipment and computers, sought donors upon returning to

America. He came back with $350,000 of used and new equipment for hospitals and schools.

The generous American and I agreed that there was more business activity and construction in 1995 than in 1993, and this continued most of the years I came. Vilnius looked increasingly prosperous. By 2001 and 2002, supermarkets had replaced the tiny, living-room-sized groceries at which we previously shopped. Indeed, one market opened two blocks from our hotel. We could then buy whatever we needed whenever we needed it. And by 2003, many buildings and sidewalks on the main street and in the Old Town had been restored to their former glory. Vilnius had gone from bleak to bright. Yet the buildings on the back streets—the places where the poor and elderly lived—were as decrepit as ever.

Collective versus Privatized Farms

My student and fellow professor, Kazys Sadauskas, and others invited our teachers to a picnic in 1995 at his summer home, a dilapidated farmhouse. What a meal we had: broiled veal on skewers, bread, sausage, herring, cheese, tomatoes, cucumbers, onions, juice, and more. Then we picked and ate wild strawberries for dessert.

Afterwards, we walked to a large, private farm, formerly a collective. Rethinking this and other experiences, I saw agriculture in Lithuania about as it was in America 50 to 60 years earlier. There were horses, wagons, and piles of hay, but few tractors. The udders of the cows were small and the farmers, I suspect, were milking by hand. Additionally, they were cutting grain and weeds with scythes. Yet they were becoming more efficient: the farmers at the collective told us that with privatization they had reduced their number of workers from 1,000 to 100.

Why Not Be Cheerful?

A college-age student, Viktorija Kelpšaitė, invited me to dinner in 2003 with her family in Kruonis. This is a town of about 2,000 people located 40 miles west of Vilnius. Her two grandmothers seemed thrilled that they could help entertain an American guest. One had been exiled to Siberia for ten years, spending much of her time sawing trees. She was a lovely, smiling, laughing, animated woman who made many gestures, slamming her hand to the table for emphasis. I asked why she was so cheerful. "Why not be cheerful?" she said. "It's no fun being sad."

Hill of Crosses

Lithuania has glorious Roman Catholic and Russian Orthodox Churches, but the most impressive religious site is the Hill of Crosses near Šiauliai. Here we found large and small crosses, crude to finely carved wooden crosses, metal crosses, and stone crosses in rows about one-half meter apart along the entire hill and its base. Many of the crosses had other crosses and rosaries hanging from them. A few were so covered with other crosses that we could not see the original cross. There were thousands, perhaps millions of crosses.

People first placed crosses on this hill in the 1800s or earlier, but the vast assembly began in the 1900s in defiance of Russian occupation. The Russians bulldozed the crosses to the ground three times—1961, 1973, and 1975—burning some and turning others to scrap metal. But the Lithuanians responded by adding more.

July 4 in Lithuania

A surprising number of Lithuanians celebrate July 4, our American Independence Day. Anyone having any connection with America wants to party. On July 4, 1996, for example, we traveled in two vans to Elektrėnai, a former communist resort some 30 miles west of Vilnius. There we joined our Lithuanian friends and a British journalist in the swimming pool and sauna. The pool had a large, fast-moving waterfall under which to stand. Also, it had two equivalents of fire hoses shooting water into the pool, and several strong underwater jets. One of our teachers nearly lost his swimming trunks under the powerful blasts! From the pool we went to a Russian sauna at 75 C (167 F), there beating ourselves with green-leaved birch branches which we thrust repeatedly into cold water. These helped us tolerate, actually enjoy the heat. Then we returned to the cold swimming pool.

After an hour of this, we gathered for dinner. Most impressive, I think, was the dessert. The English woman, Julie, had placed five flags atop the cake—four American and one British. To conclude, we all sang "Yankee Doodle," "America the Beautiful," and a lively Lithuanian tune for which we linked arms and swayed with the beat.

We switched from Elektrėnai to the American Embassy in 1997 and 1999. There was room there for perhaps 200 to 300 celebrants, American and Lithuanian, including our teachers. But the number of Americans and their friends kept growing, so the parties moved to nearby Verkių Palace in 2001 and after. We spent hours there each July eating and conversing with our friends and watching fireworks.

European Union

My young students were excited about joining the European Union. By joining it, they could eventually work anywhere in Europe. Indeed, by 2006, tens of thousands of Lithuanians were already emigrating to England and Ireland. Other Lithuanians were concerned about this loss of young workers through emigration and more concerned that joining the EU was depriving Lithuania of its recently won independence. They were also concerned about further expansion of the EU—especially if it included Turkey.

The Turkish ambassador, Kadriye Şanivar Kizildeli, and I lectured in 2006 at a leadership conference in Vilnius. She spoke gently and persuasively about the relations of Europe with Turkey. She hoped that Europeans would continue to talk with secular Turkey about their membership in the European Union, thinking this would be good for Europe and its relations with Muslim countries.

From Tribal to World View

When I was a barefoot boy in Missouri, I thought people in the eastern United States were somehow different from us—perhaps uppity, looking down their noses at us. I don't know where I got this idea. But the easterners did sound different.

When my wife and I moved to Maryland, I found I was wrong. These easterners were wonderful, good-hearted people like those in Missouri. And when we taught in China, Hungary, and Lithuania, I found the same. The people there were just as friendly as Americans and just as eager to have their children and grandchildren grow up in a world at peace.

We need to mingle, I think, with people of other nations. If we can't mingle with them, we should at least read extensively about them, trying to see the world as they see it. Why shouldn't we all have happy, fulfilling lives? Why shouldn't we all be friends?

Chapter 22.
READ EASIER STORIES

If the previous stories are too tough for your current students, try these. Here I've revised and simplified some of the stories from Chapter 21, using fewer words and shorter sentences.

If this chapter is still too hard, there's another approach. Start with children's books by Dr. Suess and similar authors, those who cleverly rhyme monosyllable words, as in *Hop on Pop*. Such books are readily available at amazon.com or amazon.co.uk or bn.com. Or try *Starfall* at starfall.com. This free, self-directing site gives easy, colorful, animated help with pronunciation, vocabulary, and reading.

What to Pack for a Trip

I met a man who had made seven trips around the world. I said, "What did you pack for your trips?" He said, "I took only one or two changes of clothes. Each night I washed what I had worn that day. Then I hung them up to dry."

I never learned to travel with so few clothes. But I did learn to pack light, and I learned to hand wash my clothes. I now travel the world with just one pack on my back. It makes it easy to get on and off planes.

Talks to Chinese

While in China, we teachers taught our classes each day and gave special talks each night. Many students came to hear us. After the talks, they came to ask questions. They talked with us for a long time. Then they walked with us to our dorm.

The students asked such questions as these: What do you like about China? Who will be the next president of the United States? How can America stop war? How can we come to study in America?

They asked our young teachers other questions: How do Americans date? How do they get married? Do you like me? Are you married? They did not say it, but I think some of them really liked our young teachers. What do you think?

Doctors Who Wave Their Hands

Some doctors in China give drugs to people who are sick. Other doctors wave their hands at them, putting their patients in a trance. These are the qigong doctors (pronounced chee-goong).

My students wanted me to see qigong doctors at work. One took me to a qigong hospital. There I spoke with doctors and patients and watched their treatments.

One patient said she had a stroke four years ago. The muscles in her right hand became so weak she could not write. But she had been treated by qigong doctors for the past month. "Now," she said, "I can write."

The head doctor then let me watch his helpers treat this patient and others. The woman first lay on her back. Then a qigong doctor waved his hands above her. This somehow put her in a trance. Her back arched, and she bounced up and down on the bed. While bouncing, her body moved toward the edge of the bed. Seeing this, the head doctor stood up and began rapidly waving his hands up and down above the woman. She then bounced back to the middle of the bed.

How does qigong work? The doctors say they pass qi (energy) through their patients, causing them to contract muscles. But they want to learn more. They want scientists to study how qigong really works.

Would You Like to Sleep in Our Tent?

Our friends in China took us to a lake high in the mountains. There we saw yurts—large, round tents—each with a Kazakh family inside. Kazakhs are a Muslim people that live in northwest China. They have sheep and ride horses. They move their tents as needed to get better grazing for their sheep.

As I walked along the lake, I saw three of these tents ahead. There were pine trees and snow on the mountain behind them. When I sat to enjoy the view, two Kazakh boys came to me. They knew only a few words of English, but we talked anyway. One leaned his head down on his hand. He was asking whether I would like to sleep that night in their tent. But I could not stay. I had to go back to teach classes.

Free Ride for Wet Americans

We teachers walked to the school where we taught in Hungary. One day five of us were caught in heavy rain as we walked home. We needed a taxi. We saw one, but it was full of people. So we jumped into the next.

The driver must have had children. We pushed away their stuffed animals to make room. Then we showed him a map and pointed to our home. He spoke little English.

When we arrived, I pulled out money. "No," he said, "No taxi!" We had mistakenly caused a kind, perhaps fearful Hungarian to give us a free ride home.

Mistakes in History

Hungarians often watch American movies. Some movies give them a wrong view of our history. One Hungarian asked one of our teachers whether she ever fought Indians. The Hungarian had no idea that our fighting stopped 100 years ago.

Americans make the same kind of mistakes. One teenage American thought Lenin Street in Szeged, Hungary, was named for John Lennon of the Beatles. She did not know it was named for Vladimir Lenin of Russia.

Russian troops left Hungary in 1991. Then the Hungarians gave Lenin Street a different name.

The Neanderthals

We took our students by train most years to a large, national park in Hungary. There we hiked through the woods to a place where we had lunch. Then we hiked to Istállóskö Cave. The students spoke English as we hiked, ate, and explored the cave.

The cave had earlier been the home of Neanderthals. This was shown by arrowheads and the bones of deer, bear, and mammoths. We could picture the Neanderthals in our minds. We could see them planning how to kill the next mammoth.

Stale Bread

János was the fun-loving driver of our van in Hungary. He spoke no English, but he waved and banged his hands as he spoke Hungarian.

János and other Hungarians love bread. Thus he was angry in Budapest when a waitress served us stale bread. He complained to her and her boss. Both said the bread was fresh.

When we returned home, János wrote to the mayor of Budapest. He told the mayor how bad the bread was. In response, the mayor had the restaurant inspected. The inspector found more problems, so the mayor closed the restaurant. It no longer exists.

Secret Police, Prison, and Siberia

The secret police (KGB) in Lithuania were brutal. We know this from what we saw and learned at the KGB prison-museum in Vilnius. We sometimes took our students there.

Our guide in 1996 and 1997 was a former prisoner who was later sent to Siberia. He showed us the small, dark cell in which he and many others stayed. He also showed us where he had to stand in a cold room over cold water until he fell asleep. Think how it felt when he fell in the water. Next he showed us where he had to sit, stand, or lie for hours without moving. Think how this felt. Then he showed us where he was questioned and beaten. But he was not angry. He just wanted to tell us the facts.

This prisoner was one of 300,000 Lithuanians sent to Siberia between 1941 and 1953. Most were teachers, lawyers, and wealthy farmers. Why did Joseph Stalin send these people to Siberia? And why were they underfed and overworked until many of them died?

Then and Now

The fear of Russia and its police in Lithuania both hurt and helped conversation. I once had lunch with Irena Veisaitė, Chair of the Open Society Fund. She said that she and her friends talked more during Soviet times. "We could not speak safely in public," she said, "so we met in our homes to discuss our feelings." She did not want to go back to those dangerous years. But she was concerned that people now work too hard, watch too much TV, and spend too much time at their computers. "We do not talk as much as we should."

Why Not Be Cheerful?

A student, Viktorija Kelpšaitė, invited me to dinner with her family. Her two grandmothers were thrilled to have an American guest, the first American they had met. One had earlier been sent to Siberia where she spent ten years sawing trees. She was a lovely, smiling, laughing woman who slammed her hand to the table for emphasis. I asked why she was so cheerful. "Why not be cheerful?" she said. "It's no fun being sad."

Hill of Crosses

Lithuania has great churches, but the best religious site is the Hill of Crosses near Šiauliai. There we found large and small crosses, wooden crosses, metal crosses, stone crosses, and others. These were lined up in rows along the hill and its base. Many of the crosses had other crosses hanging from them. A few were so covered with other crosses that we could not see the first cross. There were thousands, perhaps millions of crosses.

Most crosses were put here in the 1900s to show that people preferred their church to communism. The Russians destroyed the crosses three times: 1961, 1973, and 1975. Each time the Lithuanians put up more crosses.

European Union

Our young students were eager to join the European Union (EU). Once joined, Lithuanians could work anywhere in Europe. By 2006, tens of thousands of Lithuanians had already left for England and Ireland. Other Lithuanians were concerned about this loss of young workers. And they were more concerned that joining the EU would remove some of their hard-won freedom. Lithuania had just freed itself from Russia and the Soviet Union.

What do you think? Is Lithuania better off with the European Union or with the Soviet Union? Would it have been better yet as a separate, independent state?

Why Not be Friends?

When I was a barefoot boy in Missouri, I thought people in the eastern United States were somehow different from us. We came from simple farms and small towns. Maybe those city folk thought themselves better than us. I do not know where I got this idea. But the people from the East did sound different.

When my wife and I moved to Maryland, I found I was wrong. These were wonderful, friendly people like those I knew in Missouri.

And when we taught in China, Hungary, and Lithuania, I found the same. The people there were just as friendly as Americans. They too wanted their children to grow up in a world at peace.

We need to visit people of other nations. If we cannot visit them, we should at least read about them. We should try to see the world as they see it. Why shouldn't we all be friends? Why shouldn't we all live peaceful lives.

Chapter 23.
BUILD THEIR BRAINS

What builds the brains and minds of our children and students? And how should we change our ways of teaching to enhance this? To better understand what happens as we learn, we must look first at our nerve cells—the cells that anatomists call neurons. What are the neurons doing as we learn?

Babies and their parents, surprisingly, have about the same number of neurons (the same number of nerve cells) in their brains. But the baby neurons, unlike those in adults, have only a few branches to connect them to other neurons. Thus the babies cannot do what we adults do. Soon, however, a prodigious growing and connecting of neurons occurs. The sparsely branched neurons of babies become the many branched neurons of toddlers and preschool children. Most of this growth occurs in the cerebral cortex—the outermost, conscious part of the brain.

What spurs this branching of neurons? Most importantly, a nurturing environment. Children need nursing, touching, hugging, interaction with parents and grandparents, play with other children, running, jumping, climbing, painting, singing, dancing, stories read, and self-generated role play. They need toys too, but mainly of the simplest kind, for example, cast-off boxes for make-believe homes and shops.

As growing children increase neuronal branches in their cerebral cortices, they simultaneously increase the number of contacts between neurons. And these contacts help them remember what they have learned. This is why active participation in life brings intellectual growth.

The more variety we give our children, the keener their minds—unless we overdo it. Excessive stimulation causes stress that impedes neuronal and intellectual growth. Some parents frantically drive their children from lesson to lesson and sport to sport, stimulating them too much, leaving them little time for self-directed play and rest.

What about adults? Do enriched environments help them? Yes, indeed. The evidence comes partly from studies of rats. When young adult rats are placed as a group in a large cage filled with entertaining objects—wheels, ladders, tunnels, and such—they develop larger cerebral cortices than do rats placed individually in cages without objects. The growth results from increased neuronal size and branching in some parts of the brain and from an increased number of neurons.

So, social interaction and the presence of objects to explore and climb promote cortical growth in young rats. The investigators wondered whether it would do the same in old rats. It did. Though the response was weaker in older than in younger rats, the old cortices did benefit. The cerebral cortices of young and old alike grew thicker as neurons multiplied, branched, and connected.

Some rats died at about 600 days of age, the equivalent of about 60 years in humans. Suspecting that human contact might prolong the lives of their rats, investigators began holding them in their hands for several minutes each day after cleaning their cages. It worked! The hand-held rats survived hundreds of days longer than the others.

In short, human contact, socializing, and new activities kept the old rats alert and alive. Think how this finding might apply to older humans, perhaps to your parents or grandparents. For that matter, think how it might apply to you in the decades to come. Love, social contacts, and variety benefit all of us.

Though the studies reported here are in rats, related studies gave similar results in mice, cats, monkeys, and humans. Enrichment caused neuronal branching, connecting, and multiplying—improving memory. All of us need social, physical, and mental stimuli to thrive.

We teachers, of course, want our students to develop their brains and intellects. Since variety and social interaction promote the growth of neurons in the brain, we now know exactly how to help our students learn. We must give them variety—interestingly different, dynamic activities that stimulate their minds and bodies. And we must encourage isolated students to become more outgoing—that is, to interact frequently with other students and us.

Chapter 24.

LOVE THEM

When I first began teaching, I worked for a wise, much loved and respected chairperson—Dr. Harwell Sturdivant of Western Maryland College. I once asked him, "What is the most important of all qualities in great teachers?" I thought he would say "preparedness," for he insisted on high standards for students and teachers alike. Instead, he laid "love." To be good teachers, he felt that we must love and understand our students.

In polls of students, teachers, and college presidents, the personality or human qualities of teachers have consistently ranked high in importance. These go by various names: love, understanding, patience, sympathy, kindness, warmth, interest in students—and they are all basically synonyms for love.

It has been 50 years since Dr. Sturdivant and I discussed the importance of love and understanding, but I have never forgotten it. Teachers need other qualities for success—for example, preparedness, skill, and enthusiasm—but their love for students ties all this together.

When Dr. Sturdivant said "love your students," I pondered how best to do this. While pondering, I thought of Shakespeare who said, "They do not love who do not show their love." I concluded that a loving teacher—or a loving person of any kind—should be friendly, helpful, and interested in other people. And when we show our love in this manner, our students, in turn, love us and respond well to our teaching.

When I later became chair of the sciences at a different location, Grand Canyon College, I applied Dr. Sturdivant's "love and understanding" to our faculty and students. We were a tiny department in those days, only 40 undergraduate majors in science and a half dozen or so professors. But by using love, intense recruiting, and other methods, we grew in 11 years from 40 to 605 majors. Had our professors kept distant from students, drawn only to academics, our recruiting would surely have failed. Well-qualified students seek empathetic professors who push them to do their best. Our professors did that. They pushed them but also gave them the time, encouragement, and love they deserved.

My wife and I left our office doors open for students and urged others to do likewise. Thus we had frequent visitors, more yet because our offices were next to a couch-filled lobby. A few of us ate brown-bag lunches with our students in the lobby.

Our world is sometimes harsh, but we can make it pleasant for our students and others through little acts of love. And these acts generate ripples, spreading the love to others.

Chapter 25.
GET ENTHUSED

Whatever you do in life, do it with gusto, do it with enthusiasm, pour your heart into it. If you are a teacher, be enthusiastic. If you are a writer, be enthusiastic. If you are the designer of an assembly-line car, such as the Model T Ford, be enthusiastic. As Henry Ford said, "Enthusiasm is at the bottom of all progress."

How powerful is enthusiasm? I have a friend, Maida Navis, who will show you. She inspired me as never before or since by her own contagious enthusiasm and good deeds. While living in Colorado, Maida learned of a hungry woman and child who walked five miles to a welfare office only to be told that there was no food available until the next day. The woman fainted while walking home.

Hearing this, Maida got busy. She immediately took groceries to the woman and her family. Then she began speaking day after day at churches, schools, businesses, clubs, and other organizations, seeking donations for similar families. Indeed, she gave 226 talks to such groups during her first year. She and Warren, her husband, filled their garage with donated food, clothing, and furniture.

The group founded by Maida—the Inter-Faith Task Force—gave help immediately to all who asked. If families needed food, volunteers took it; if children needed clothing for school or adults needed clothing for new jobs, they got it; if children needed day care while their mothers worked, the group gave it; if older people needed transportation, hot lunches, or repairs to their homes, volunteers did it; if families needed furniture, volunteers delivered it.

To help finance the Task Force, Maida organized yearly walks of 25 miles. The walkers got businesses and others to pay her group if they completed the walk. Soon she had thousands of high-school students and others making these long but exciting treks. She did it too and had blisters to prove it.

Within seven years, Maida had 10,000 volunteers helping. How could she do so much so quickly? The answer: enthusiasm—contagious enthusiasm. She felt strongly that this was the right thing to do, compelling her to speak forcefully. Businesses as well as individuals gave whatever she asked, including a building for classrooms, offices, and storage, and ten vans for transporting people and goods.

Maida's volunteers taught four preschools. The classes were held in brightly colored rooms filled with toys, books, crayons, paper, and more, but the children, being poor and sometimes abused, responded differently from other children. A teacher once asked her class how many had breakfast that morning. To her surprise, some didn't know the meaning of breakfast.

Maida's enthusiasm carried her further. She and her group organized summer camps for children, classes for their parents, and a children's choir with about 60 members, a choir that sang to audiences of up to 1,000 people. Imagine the joy the children felt as they sang. And imagine the joy they spread with their youthful voices.

In sum, Maida and her helpers became near saints for the indigent. Perhaps this is best told by a former alcoholic, a man who lost his job and pride and, in a fit of remorse, shot himself in the stomach. Gene Jarrell quotes his letter in *One Woman, Never Alone*:

"We owe, I owe, you and your organization so very, very much for the fight that you helped me to win. When, if ever, you should doubt yourself or your organization's accomplishments, . . . remember what you have done for me and mine. Five (5) people . . . real human beings lifted from the slums . . . raised from the gloom and depression of alcoholism, from moral and financial poverty by you and your fellow workers. . . . I can now look life and people straight in the eye!

"I know that when judgment comes and I see God in heaven that on his right hand side will stand Maida and her followers and they will be wearing tennis shoes in preparation for the last Walk."

If you ever doubt what one enthusiastic, determined person can do—remember Maida.

Chapter 26.

QUIZ THEM

How well do our students speak, write, and understand English? We learn this after a few days in class, but it's better to know from the start. If you have only a few students, you can learn their abilities simply by speaking with them. If you have more, you may want to give them an oral or written quiz.

Here's a quiz similar to that our teachers give at our first meeting with incoming students. Let's say we have 50 students of widely varying ability to assign to five teachers. By giving and grading the quiz, we can tell which students to put in which classes: beginning, intermediate, or advanced. The quiz isn't perfect, so we let the students shift classes later if they and their teachers think it best.

You may also want each new student to compose two or three sentences in English, giving you an even better look at their potential. I sometimes ask, "What do you want to learn from your English class?"

Perhaps you already know the approximate abilities of your incoming students. If most or all are beginners in English, ask them only the easier questions from the early part of this quiz. Beginners get discouraged when asked a long series of questions for which they have no answers.

In contrast, if you know that all of your students are advanced, don't give the quiz. I skipped the quiz in 2011, for example, because all of my students were Lithuanian teachers of English. They took my class to get additional ideas for teaching their classes.

Directions. Have your students read and simultaneously listen to these or similar questions. Your voice may sound different from British or American voices the students have heard before, causing them concern. But they will quickly adapt to your voice and other new voices during the first days of class.

I read each question to the students twice. Better yet, I some-times read a question and then have another teacher repeat the same question. By hearing two different voices—preferably one male and one female—the student can more easily understand the questions.

Speak clearly and somewhat more slowly than usual. There's no reason to scare off beginners with rapid-fire speech. You may return to your normal rate of speech later, that is, after students become adapt-ed to your voice.

When grading the quiz, accept alternative answers if warranted, giving either full or half credit.

1. What is your name?
2. How many eyes do you have?
3. How many fingers are on one of your hands?
4. What is the color of human blood?
5. What does a pilot fly?
6. In what do fish swim?
7. What is the largest city in England?
8. What season of the year is the hottest?
9. What do you do with a pencil?
10. In what country is Tokyo located?
11. What nation is located directly north of the United States?
12. In what room of a house do we usually find a sink, refrigerator, and stove?
13. What do people insert in a lock to open a door?
14. With what utensil do people cut meat at a dinner table?
15. What number do I get when I subtract 9 from 12?
16. What do we find on the shelves of a library?
17. What do I call the father of my mother?
18. While walking north, I come to a corner and turn right. What direction am I now walking?
19. Pretend that it is now 9:45 a.m. What time will it be one-half hour from now?
20. What is the name of the pet that barks and pants?
21. What is the largest living mammal?
22. What is the largest of the 50 states in the United States?
23. What is a synonym for obese?

Write the correct word or words to replace each of the under-lined words in the following sentences:

24. <u>Me</u> cried but she laughed.
25. <u>Them</u> bottles were full.
26. We don't have <u>nobody</u> to go there.
27. What had he been <u>do</u>?
28. Let's <u>except</u> their invitation to dinner.
29. She <u>will go</u> to the bank yesterday.
30. <u>Their</u> going to class.

Chapter 27.
GO TO THE WEB

There are brilliant, gold-vein resources for teaching English, and, others dull as dirt. Even the gold gets tarnished at times by distracting ads, for example, those with flashing red lights. The gold you seek is that which works best for your level of students: beginning, intermediate, or advanced. This list of websites will help you find it.

A+ Research & Writing for High School and College Students at ipl. org/div/aplus gives step-by-step directions for researching and writing papers.

Activities for ESL Students at a4esl.org gives grammar and vocabulary quizzes, crossword puzzles, and audio and video activities taught by different speakers of English. The speakers talk at slower-than-usual rates, making it easier for inexperienced students to understand.

Amazon at amazon.com or amazon.co.uk and *Barnes and Noble* at bn.com have millions of books, new and used, many with reviews and sample pages to read.

BBC Learning English at bbclearningenglish.com provides many choices from news to grammar to quizzes to lesson plans.

EDSITEment at edsitement.neh.gov offers the "best of the humanities." Once there, click either FEATURES, LESSON PLANS, STUDENT RESOURCES, Art & Culture, Foreign Language, History & Social Studies, or Literature & Language Arts.

EFL/ESL Lessons and Lesson Plans at iteslj.org/Lessons is a vast source of thought-provoking lessons published in the *Internet TESL Journal.*

The EFL Playhouse at esl4kids.net works well for teachers and their beginning students of any age. Click on chants, fingerplays, games, interactive puzzles and quizzes, phonics and phonemic awareness, printable materials, songs, teaching tips, tongue twisters, or links.

elllo at elllo.org is a fascinating site. English speakers from around the world describe various topics as students listen, read along, and occasionally click answers to questions.

English Comes Alive! at englishcomesalive.com is a supplement to the book you are now reading, a source of lively ideas for teachers of ESL and EFL.

Google Books at books.google.com—an online library—provides text from millions of books, both fiction and nonfiction. Many of the books are free.

Google at google.com is the most used, most reliable of all search engines. Type keywords, such as ESL or EFL, into its search box, and hit the enter key to find the information you seek. For special searches, click images, videos, maps, news, gmail, or more, before entering your keywords.

Howjsay at howjsay.com is a talking dictionary that pronounces the English words you type or click, defines them, gives examples of their use in sentences, and translates them into other languages.

Listen and Read at spotlightradio.net/listen has speakers reading easy but interesting stories at slower than usual rates. They speak as you read.

ManyThings at manythings.org provides well-written activities for English practice outside class: stories to hear and simultaneously read, flash quizzes, crossword puzzles, and much more.

Merriam-Webster at merriam-webster.com has a dictionary and thesaurus. Click the speaker icon to hear pronunciation.

The Purdue Online Writing Lab (OWL) at owl.english.purdue.edu lists ESL resources, explains grammar, and gives excellent advice for writers.

Starfall at starfall.com entertainingly prods children and beginning ESL students to learn English online. The lessons are colorful, animated, and verbal—giving your students memorable practice with pronunciation and vocabulary.

Voice of America at voanews.com lets students simultaneously read and listen to a broad range of news. Once there, click News, Programs, Video, and, most important, Learning English.

Web English Teacher at webenglishteacher.com lists its contents as Children's Literature, ENL/ESL, Grammar, Poetry, Reading/Literacy, Speech, Vocabulary, and Writing, among others.

Wikipedia at wikipedia.org is a free, web-based encyclopedia containing millions of English articles written by volunteers. Scroll to the bottom of its homepage for other free products, for example, a *Wiktionary* (dictionary and thesaurus).

THANK YOU, COLLEAGUES

Wendy Clark, thanks for letting me teach your opening-day EFL class in China. If you hadn't galloped off with the Kazakh to drink mare's milk, you wouldn't have gotten sick, and I wouldn't have taught your delightful students. You and the Kazakh led me to an exciting career.

Treva Gibson, you too deserve a toast in mare's milk, but let's make it pasteurized. Thanks for getting me the grant to teach in China, for training me in ESL, and for selecting me as the leader of our teachers in Hungary while you zipped off to Russia. As the Director of International Studies at Grand Canyon University, you helped many of us become teachers of English in China, Hungary, and Lithuania.

Sandor Klein, thanks for steering over 200 students into our native-speaker English courses in Szeged, Hungary, and for introducing our teachers to those of the American Studies Department in Eger.

Lehel Vadon, thanks for opening the first ever American Studies Department in Hungary and for inviting our group to teach your students at Esterházy Károly College. Thus began our year-after-year, highly informative exchange of teachers and students between Arizona and Hungary.

Thanks also, Lehel, for listening to our occasional complaints about Hungarian summers. In response, you sent us 600 miles north for a meeting with your friend, Irena Navickienė. Soon our teachers were presenting English in both warm Hungary and cool Lithuania.

Thank you, Irena, for accepting our teachers at Vilnius Pedagogical University. You've worked with us now for nearly two decades. These have been heart-warming, instructive years for our dozens of teachers and their hundreds of Lithuanian students taking English.

Thanks to all the dedicated, enthusiastic teachers who made our programs in China and Europe so successful. Some taught multiple summers: Treva Gibson, C. J. Stevens, Judi and Pete Hermann, Jane

117

Preston, Doug and Sophie Pease, Stephanie Pease, Erdie Morris, Dawn Barnier, Peggy Linkin, Bob and Ilene Berg, Mary Harris, and my wife, Becky Witherspoon.

We teachers ate most meals together, partly to tell each other what worked best in our classes, but mostly because we loved being together. I wish you readers could have been with us: sharing stories, sharing lessons, and sharing the humor of each day until tears ran down our cheeks.

Two of these EFL teachers also served as editors for this book, *English Comes Alive!* Thank you, Judi Hermann and Becky Witherspoon. You've been a tremendous help.

ABOUT THE AUTHOR

Mare's milk drew Dr. Witherspoon to the teaching of English, contaminated mare's milk. A colleague in China drank it, got a temperature of 104º F, and temporarily gave her class to him. He loved both the subject and the students. So he later took a course in teaching ESL and soon became a recruiter and leader for groups of English teachers going overseas.

He has now taught seven summers in Hungary and twelve in Lithuania, bringing other teachers with him. As the leader during most of these years, he collected and devised rousing, easily remembered activities to present both to his students and fellow teachers. This book is the end product.

To learn more about the author and his ideas for teaching ESL/EFL, or to e-mail him, go to www.englishcomesalive.com.

Other Books: Witherspoon taught biology before English, so his earlier books, audiovisuals, and computer programs are mainly in that field. They include: *The Living Laboratory* (Doubleday), *The Functions of Life* (Addison-Wesley), *Human Physiology* (Harper & Row), and *From Field to Lab* (TAB McGraw-Hill).

INDEX

English Comes Alive!

English Comes Alive!

English Comes Alive!

126